More than PETTICOATS

REMARKABLE MAINE WOMEN

Kate Kennedy

TWODOT®

GUILFORD, CONNECTICUT
HELENA, MONTANA
AN IMPRINT OF THE GLOBE PEQUOT PRESS

For my mom and game gal extraordinaire,
Nancy Elliott Kennedy

A · T W O D O T ® · B O O K

Copyright © 2005 by The Globe Pequot Press

All rights reserved. No part of this book may be reproduced or transmitted in any form by any means, electronic or mechanical, including photocopying and recording, or by any information storage and retrieval system, except as may be expressly permitted by the 1976 Copyright Act or by the publisher. Requests for permission should be made in writing to The Globe Pequot Press, P.O. Box 480, Guilford, Connecticut 06437.

TwoDot is a registered trademark of The Globe Pequot Press.

Map by Sue Cary © The Globe Pequot Press

Library of Congress Cataloging-in-Publication Data
Kennedy, Kate, 1948-
    More than petticoats. Remarkable Maine women/Kate Kennedy.—1st ed.
        p. cm.—(More than petticoats series)
    Includes bibliographical references and index
    ISBN 0-7627-3147-8
        I. Women—Maine—Biography. 2. Women—Maine—History. 3. Maine—
    Biography. I. Title: Remarkable Maine women. II. Title. III. Series.

CT3262.M2K46 2005
920.72'09741—dc22
[B]
                                                                        2005040412

Manufactured in the United States of America
First Edition/First Printing

CONTENTS

Acknowledgments

Thank you, Cally Gurley and Jennifer Tuttle of the Maine Women Writers Collection at the University of New England, for your rich resources and encouraging words; crew of the Thomas Memorial Library in Cape Elizabeth, for smiling through countless interlibrary loans; staff at the Maine Historical Society and Maine Memory Network, in particular Bill Barry and Candace Kanes, for passionately animating the past. Thank you, Megan Hiller, for manuscript tips and day-one enthusiasm; David Kuchta and Jennifer Tuttle for your willingness to read a draft *in toto* and write useful tandem margin notes. Thank you, Stephanie Hester, for top-notch editing, as well as for your good senses of both humor and perspective.

For help with individual chapters, I'm very grateful to experts of every ilk—writers, historians, and families—who have shared their knowledge, photos, and sometimes memories of the women presented here: Geraldine Chassé, Rhéa Côté Robbins, March O. McCubrey, Charles N. Shay, Emma Nicolar, Caron Shay, Bunny McBride, Dahlov Ipcar, Peggy Zorach, Jessica Nicoll, June McKenzie, Michele McKenzie, Merita McKenzie, Phyllis Rogers, and the Sabbathday Lake Society of Shakers and its library staff.

Always, daily thank-yous to my kind, stalwart, inspiring friends and extended family, especially to the four lively generations of Kennedy/Greene/Burke/Ray/Abel/Vidor girls and women. And thank you, Rachel K. Greene, for growing up so beautifully, even with a writer for a mom, and Nate Greene, for twenty-five years of laughter and life support, including the dollars-for-chapters scheme.

Madawaska

CANADA

St John River

Caribou
Fort Fairfield

**Aroostook
County**

CANADA

Eagle Lake

Houlton

▲ *Mount
Katahdin*

Moosehead Lake

Kennebec River

M A I N E

Penobscot River

Dover-Foxcroft

*Flagstaff
Lake*

*Wyman
Lake*

Rangeley
Lakes

Indian Island
Orono
Bangor

Phillips

Skowhegan

Farmington

Augusta

Lincolnville
Beach

Rockland

*Penobscot
Bay*

Shaker
Village

Lewiston

Brunswick   Bath

Matinicus Rock

A T L A N T I C

*Sebago
Lake*

*Casco
Bay*

*Robinhood
Cove*

O C E A N

Portland
Scarborough

Alfred

S. Berwick

NEW HAMPSHIRE

N

0   Miles   50

0   Kilometers   50

Introduction

The older I get, the more the enthusiasms of my girlhood well up: bugs, biographies, word-origins, being outside. With a cereal spoon, I used to dig up ant colonies and resettle them in my mother's Pyrex casserole. At the library, I'd dig into the lives of Sacajawea, Mozart, Marie Antoinette, Dolley Madison. It tickled me that "hippopotamus" meant "river horse." I climbed trees and rode my bike, hell-bent, feeling pockets of air change temperature when I streaked through, smelling leaf mold, seaweed, and *Rosa rugosa.* My friend Connie the Bold and I broke into houses under construction, then, rubber-booted, splashed in a nearby brook. I pretended to be Navajo. I pretended to speak French.

Marguerite Yourcenar, the great French novelist and first woman elected to the Académie Française (and resident of Mt. Desert Island, Maine, from 1950 until her death in 1987), called such enthusiasms "affinities." For her, these meant the fictional or historical characters that suddenly inhabited her and demanded voice. In my trusty Skeat etymological dictionary, I see that "affinity" comes from the Latin "ad" (*to* or *near*) and "finis" (*an end* or *boundary*). To me, then, an affinity draws us close enough to people—or to animals, books, ideas, landscapes—to touch them, to share a common boundary.

For some of the women in these pages, I felt an instant affinity. For others, the connection of interest and empathy took longer to spark. It grew out of digging not only into the facts of their lives but into the histories of the boreal forests, the villages and farms, the cities, lakes and rivers, the granite islands that helped to forge them. Of these thirteen remarkable Maine women, all born before 1900, six lived to be over ninety. Their birth dates span more than 150 years; the distance between their homes stretches as far as 400 miles, from South Berwick, near New Hampshire, to Madawaska, along Maine's boundary with New Brunswick, Canada. Avant-garde painter, botanist, lighthouse keeper, fly-fishing journalist, U.S. senator, social reformer, fiction writer, clairvoyant, Shaker singer, midwife, Penobscot Indian basketmaker, opera diva, Arctic explorer: What I found is everything my girlhood-self wanted to be, and what my adult-self still greatly admires.

I've lived in Maine year-round for twenty-eight years, and for twenty-one years before that I spent a few weeks on a coastal island each summer. I knew a smattering of Maine history: its logging, seafaring, and fishing legacies; its uneasy relationship with its original inhabitants, the Passamaquoddies, Penobscots, and Maliseets. I knew about the ongoing tug-of-war between conserving and exploiting the state's fresh and saltwater riches, its forestlands, its vibrant human resources, as well. But I knew few particulars—including the yeasty, inspiring, eccentric, astounding personal stories of its women.

When my ninety-year-old mother says of a friend or acquaintance, "She's a game gal," I know it's high praise. To me the expression has always conjured a certain kind of bravery—bold high spirits in the face of hardship and heartache, as well as the self-sufficiency to create a meaningful life for oneself, no matter what. These are Maine virtues, shared by the women in this book, and by so many others there was not space or time enough to explore: the young women from Quebec whose long hours of labor for pennies at Maine's leather and textile factories equipped the Union army during the Civil War; the Irish and Italian immigrants, the Jews from Eastern Europe whose hard work, high hopes, and vitality energized Maine's cities and towns.

The nineteenth-century Maine writer Sarah Orne Jewett believed it was important to see for herself the houses and haunts of women she admired. After visiting Charlotte and Emily Bronte's home by the Yorkshire moors, she wrote, "You always find something of what made them the souls they were, and, at any rate, you see their sky and their earth." I've taken her advice. In researching these women's lives, I tried to gulp as much of "their sky and their earth" as I could. In late June, I saw where Tante Blanche crossed the St. John River, fleeing persecution by the English. It was a bright, warm early October afternoon when I walked into the Bowdoin College Library and opened the folios of Kate Furbish's botanic paintings—as brightly colored and full-of-life as when she created them in the 1870s. Later that same month maple leaves flamed up red and yellow when I drove to the saltwater farm where artist Marguerite Zorach did much of her work. I touched the wallpaper she'd hand painted, admired the blue-green and gold view of Robinhood Cove that so inspired her. In December, during a snowstorm, I crossed the bridge over the Penobscot River that Florence Nicolar Shay had helped to build. Her son, Charles Shay, showed me ash-splint baskets his mother had woven, and I sat in a chair where she had sat. I walked to Green Memorial AME Zion Church on Portland's Munjoy Hill, as Florence Eastman Williams used to do, and I stood in the workroom at the Sabbathday Lake Shaker Village where Sister Mildred Barker dipped chocolates by hand and taught other sisters the extraordinary heritage of Shaker songs.

I hope in reading these biographies you'll develop your own affinities and want to learn more about some of these women, as well as the many not written about here. Resources abound, from women's-history walking trails to Web sites, from historical societies and libraries to the amazing memory treasure-troves our mothers, grandmothers, neighbors, and friends can offer if we just ask for their stories.

INTRODUCTION

In a 1947 essay entitled "The Heart and the Lyre," Maine poet and literary critic Louise Bogan detailed what she felt was the task ahead for women poets. Her words, as apt now as they must have been then, chart a course not just for future writers. They distill what this baker's dozen of "game gals" has meant to me:

> . . . at the moment, in a time lacking in truth and certainty and filled with anguish and despair, no woman should be shamefaced in attempting to give back to the world, through her work, a portion of its lost heart.

MARGUERITE-BLANCHE THIBODEAU CYR
(1738–1810)

Tante Blanche:
The Mother of Madawaska

In 1797, violent winter storms flung snow and sleet against the logs of an isolated, rough-hewn cabin in northernmost Maine. Snow devoured carefully stacked woodpiles and mounded over small, canvas-covered windows. It seethed like sand under the plank door. Alone inside, fifty-nine-year-old Tante (Aunt) Blanche—healer, midwife, pioneer—fed logs to the fire and prayed. Christened Marguerite-Blanche Thibodeau, Marguerite was called "Tante Blanche" by family, neighbors, and friends as a sign of both affection and honor. True to her nature, she didn't dwell on her own plight; instead, her thoughts traveled across snow-swept fields and woods into other isolated cabins. There, painful scenes awaited her mind's eye: Members of the small, tightly knit community of French-speaking settlers—some her own children and grandchildren—were slowly dying of starvation.

Twice in her lifetime, Tante Blanche and her family had been expelled from Nova Scotia and New Brunswick by colonial British troops, and they'd wandered for years, searching for a place to live

PHOTO BY STEVE YOUNG

Carving of "The Arrival of Tante Blanche" by Maine artist Claude "Blackie" Cyr

in peace. With backbreaking work, they had carved a new colony out of the wilderness on the banks of the St. John River (part of Maine's present-day boundary with New Brunswick, Canada). But now it wasn't war that endangered them. For two years in a row, fall floods and killing frosts had decimated their crops. In 1797—the Year of the Black Famine—2 inches of snow fell in early September so that there was pitifully little to harvest. The settlers had no reserves, and the faraway government of New Brunswick had not yet helped with supplies. Anticipating disaster, some families abandoned their log cabins and traveled down the St. John River toward Fredericton. Most, however, decided to stay. They had spent years buffeted by war; what they desired above all else was to farm their own lands in peace.

It was a winter scoured by deep privation. At first, the pioneers lived on small game and whatever wild herbs they'd managed to gather. But even those food sources quickly ran out. Soon the last milk cow was slaughtered and eaten, the last boiled wheat licked from bowls. In desperation, a group of men set off to hunt moose, caribou, bear, deer, rabbit—whatever animals they could find in the snowy forests and along the frozen river. Among the hunting party was Joseph Cyr, Tante Blanche's husband.

After the men left, it began to snow in earnest. For eight days and nights, a blizzard raged. Many women, already sick with malnutrition, could not take care of themselves or their babies. Tables lay bare. Cabins grew colder and colder since tending a fire required a strength they no longer possessed. Children wailed, their bellies filled only with air. And still the hunters did not return.

Snowbound in her own cabin, Tante Blanche pondered all of this. Blessed with robust good health, she herself did not get sick, but she felt the full weight of responsibility for those less fortunate than she. Tante Blanche was a leader in her settlement, endowed with a natural aptitude and interest, and trained through years of experience to prepare home remedies and to help women in childbirth. Related to many settlers through birth or marriage, she couldn't just stand by and watch their dreams—and her own—expire. She was a devout Roman Catholic who'd prayed for her community's deliverance, but prayer was not enough: She needed to take action. And so she did. First, the search for any stores of wheat and barley she might have overlooked, any stray potatoes, bits of cured meat, or uneaten root vegetables. These she bundled into pockets and leather pouches. Then she gathered every piece of warm clothing she could spare. She took down her snowshoes, strapped them onto her boots, and headed out into the storm, dragging behind her a heavy wooden sled, loaded with provisions.

The wind blew so hard it was difficult to find her way. She could barely even see the sled or the bear-paw prints her snowshoes made before they too were swallowed up. At times, earth and sky felt like one: stinging white, and bitter, bitter cold. For hours she tramped over hills, through heavy forest, across cleared fields where frozen crops lay buried under tons of ice and snow. At each cabin, she stopped to offer help. Depending on what was needed, she delivered bits of meat and grain, homemade herbal medicines, or furs to use as blankets. From the cabins of wealthier settlers, she begged any supplies they could spare, which she then distributed to the next desperate family.

Most of the cabins were single rooms made of round logs, caulked with moss, then covered with birch bark. Using her healing skills, she nursed settlers too sick to move. Inside some homes, an infant or a grandparent had already died of starvation. Here Tante Blanche stayed to lay out the dead and to pray with grieving families; then she cooked for them and urged them to eat. Along her route, she also carried intangibles as important as food: hope, faith, and health.

At last, after eight days, the snow let up and the hunters struggled back. So terrible had been their ordeal that one of them had died from exposure and another was near death. But they brought meat, and the Madawaska colony was saved. For her own brave efforts in saving the community, Tante Blanche was hailed as a hero.

By the time Marguerite-Blanche Thibodeau was born in 1738 at Beaubassin (now the city of Amherst, Nova Scotia), France and England had been fighting off and on for more than one hundred years. The prize: possession of North America. The daughter of Jean-Baptiste Thibodeau and Marie LeBlanc, Marguerite grew up immersed in French traditions. She spoke the French of her ancestors, attended Mass at the local Catholic church, and helped with farming and household chores. Her family's homeland, called "Acadia" and ruled by France, had been a vast territory that included the present-day Canadian provinces of Nova Scotia, New Brunswick, and Prince Edward Island, as well as parts of Quebec and the State of Maine. Although the Treaty of Utrecht, signed in 1713 at the end of Queen Anne's War, had officially granted all of Canada to England—including Acadia—this seems to have had little direct effect on Marguerite's childhood, in spite of her family's having had to swear nominal allegiance to England.

However, in 1755, when she was seventeen, Marguerite's relatively stable world turned upside down. In that year—during the French and Indian War—the British demanded that Acadians strictly abide by the terms of the forty-two-year-old Treaty of Utrecht. This meant signing a new oath of allegiance, not only swearing loyalty to King George II but also agreeing to take up arms against any French settlers who might threaten English authority. Many Acadians, including Marguerite's father, refused to do this.

The British reprisal was swift and brutal. Marguerite's family, along with approximately 6,000 other men, women, and children, were forced from their homes. Colonial British troops, posted in New England, deported some of the Acadians to American colonies further south. Families were separated—women from their husbands, fathers from their children—and all of their property was confiscated. Some Acadian settlements, such as Grand Pré, were burned to the ground. Families were terrorized, and the churches, houses, and farms they'd struggled to create were destroyed. And so began years of displacement and wandering. A real-life survivor of this violent upheaval, Marguerite lived many of the events dramatized by Maine's poet Henry Wadsworth Longfellow in his tragic romantic epic about the Great Expulsion, "Evangeline," published in 1847. Marguerite's grandfather, René LeBlanc, was the notary public of Grand Pré, whom Longfellow's poem immortalized.

In 1755, Marguerite and her family fled north to a small Acadian settlement on the southern shore of the St. Lawrence River, called St. Louis de Kamouraska, about 100 miles from

Quebec City. In 1760, Marguerite married Joseph-François Cyr, also from Beaubassin. Three years older than Marguerite, Joseph was one of eleven children—two daughters and nine sons—of Jean-Baptiste Cyr and Ann-Marguerite Cormier. His family had known the same heartache and trauma as hers. Marguerite and Joseph shared not only an abiding, pragmatic love but a common culture and history. Their first child, named Marguerite Cyr, was born in May of 1761 at St. Louis de Kamouraska. A son followed a year and a half later, in November of 1762. But tragedy struck in February of 1763 when both children died within two days of each other from an unidentified illness. In spite of these terrible losses, life moved on, and Marguerite gave birth to three more sons: Joseph in June of 1764; Firmin in April of 1766; and Jean-Baptiste in 1767.

Because of sporadic harassment from the English, Marguerite, her husband, and his extended family kept searching for land to cultivate far from any colonial conflict. They settled in Ekoupag (now Maugerville, New Brunswick), up the St. John River from Fredericton, in wilderness territory. Here they farmed rich land on the river. Here also Marguerite's youngest son, Jean-Baptiste, died in early childhood. In 1770, Marguerite gave birth to a daughter, Théotiste Marie, and two years later a son, Pierre Hilarion, was born. Of her seven children, born over an eleven-year span, only four lived into adulthood. For mothers on the frontier, hardships were many; surely the untimely deaths of children must have been the worst.

In 1783, at the end of the American Revolution, more political trouble erupted for Marguerite and her family. Settlers from the thirteen American colonies still loyal to the British crown found themselves unwelcome in the new United States, and they emigrated to southern New Brunswick and Nova Scotia. Governor Carleton of Nova Scotia confiscated Acadian farms, including those of the Cyrs. In 1784, he granted these lands to members of the Second Battalion of Volunteers of New Jersey as well as to a regiment of American Dragoons. Acadians' petitions for the return of their farms were ignored. They had no choice but to abandon their most recent settlement and move on, yet again.

In 1784 and 1785, Marguerite's husband, eight brothers-in-law, and father-in-law wrote to the Governor-General of Canada requesting land grants in the Madawaska Territory. Each head of household eventually received 200 acres and some supplies to forge yet another settlement. Old Jean-Baptiste Cyr, by this time in his late seventies, bowed by hardship and injustice, is said to have walked his farmland in Ekoupag one last time before leaving it forever. "My God!" he cried, "Can it be true that there is no place left on earth for a cayen [Acadian]?"

In all, twenty-four families asked for land a mile and a half below the Great Falls on the St. John River. In June of 1785, Marguerite saw her new land for the first time. What she found was rich, hilly country, much of it blanketed by tall trees, with mountains rising in the distance. Tall grass and wild hay covered much of the marshy lowlands, good feed for the animals that were to arrive that fall, sent up from Ekoupag. When she first set foot on the southern bank of the St. John, Marguerite was forty-seven years old. She and Joseph, some of their surviving children, and her husband's family were all starting over.

That first year, they pooled their belongings, helped each other clear land, and planted potatoes along with a few acres of wheat. In the winter, the men tended trap lines and spent days at lumber camps, felling trees which they would float down the St. John once the ice thawed. English shipbuilders along the coast eagerly awaited the tall straight trees for use as masts for sailing ships. In March and April, the settlers boiled down water-thin sap to make maple syrup. There was no wool in the early years of the colony: All clothes were made from fur and leather. During the summer the colonists, using oxen, cleared acres of forest, and they cultivated crops for export, as well as for their own needs. They grew enough wheat and barley to ship some down-river to Fredericton, where the grain market was brisk.

In spite of occasional boundary disputes between New Brunswick and Quebec—as well as the United States—over who controlled the Madawaska Territory, life was fairly peaceful and prosperous for Marguerite, far better than it had been closer to the seat of the British colonial government. All four of her remaining children married between the years 1791 and 1795, and she was soon a grandmother. Even before her heroism during the Black Famine, Marguerite was well known as both a midwife and a healer. By all accounts, she was a formidable woman, strong in body and character.

Thomas Albert, in his book *The History of Madawaska*, wrote:

When all of Tante Blanche's works of mercy became known, she became the focus of a universal veneration that bordered on adoration. She was believed to cure the sick, remove curses, find lost objects, reconcile enemies, and bring good luck. Her greatest asset was bringing the most hardened sinner back to a most exemplary life of piety. Her severe rebukes—and if these did not suffice, the threat of her formidable fist—were enough to change the most habitual drunkard, who feared her more than the bishop.

Tante Blanche's husband, Joseph Cyr, died in 1803 or 1804. At the end of her own days, she was living in another St. John Valley settlement, Van Buren, where she died on March 29, 1810, at the age of seventy-two. Tante Blanche was buried across the river in the

Catholic parish church at St. Basile (now part of New Brunswick, Canada). This would have been an almost unheard-of honor for any layman; for a woman it was an unprecedented homage.

Many of the St. John Valley's Franco-American residents still speak French as their first language and can trace their ancestry back to Tante Blanche and even beyond, to villages in France. To honor and preserve its bicultural heritage, Madawaska has "French days" when shopkeepers, town employees, and regular citizens are urged to speak their mother tongue. The region still celebrates Acadian festivals and each summer hosts huge Franco-American family reunions.

Down river from Madawaska, in nearby St. David, the 1969 Madawaska Centennial Log Cabin, now named The Tante Blanche Historic Museum, houses artifacts from colonial days, donated to the Madawaska Historical Society. Just behind the museum, on the banks of the St. John, is the site where the original Acadian settlers first crossed over into the new world they would finally call their permanent home, thanks to Tante Blanche's formidable heroism and charity—and perhaps strong fist.

For generations the oral history of Tante Blanche's deeds has been passed down from grandparent to grandchild in the St. John Valley. By birth and by marriage, she was an actual aunt to many young Acadian colonists. To everyone she was an honorary aunt, or, as she's sometimes called, "la vraie mère (the true mother) de Madawaska." Marguerite-Blanche Thibodeau Cyr, a true daughter of political, cultural, and religious turmoil, displaced time and again, managed to transcend the tragedies visited upon her, transforming her life into an enduring symbol of generosity and strength.

KATE FURBISH

(1834–1931)

Botanic Artist in the Garden of Maine

*I*t was a cool fall morning in 1882, and the trees of Aroostook County in northeastern Maine blazed with red and yellow leaves. Here in the wilderness, far from any city, Kate Furbish was collecting plant specimens, alone. She hadn't found anyone to go with her, but there was nothing unusual about that. Often this tiny, forty-eight-year-old woman tramped through marshes and across mountains by herself and without a thought, in search of new wildflowers, ferns, trees, mushrooms—whatever the natural world would offer up. She especially liked watery places and the plants that grew there, from pitcher plants to sundews and leather leaf.

On this particular morning, Kate was headed toward a large pond she hadn't yet explored. While climbing a wet ravine, she was delighted to find iron pyrites embedded in the surrounding slate. Using a hammer and chisel she carried in a basket on her back, she stopped to chip off several pounds of the brassy metallic crystals. These she put in the basket, along with the tools, her lunch, an insect net and bottles, and a vasculum—a box for holding newly

Kate Furbish

collected plant specimens. Soon the bank grew very steep. Kate was so focused on reaching the pond, though, that she never considered turning back. First she lifted the basket over her head and placed it above her on the bank, not far from her top leg. Her lower leg balanced on a fallen tree. Just as she pushed off, the rotten wood gave way and her whole leg was buried. Above her, the basket. Below her, sharp rocks. As she wondered how to free herself, the basket and its contents fell down, hitting her face and shoulder, and clattering into the ravine.

By this time, Kate hurt all over, but there was no one to turn to but herself. Summoning her strength, she tried to leap by throwing her weight on her free leg and then springing up. Unfortunately, the earth crumbled even more. Now she was buried up to her waist. While she rested for a short time, she planned her escape. Finally, with great effort, she managed to extricate herself. Then, after gathering up the contents of her basket, she climbed the bank again and hurried on to the pond. Eleven hours after she'd left that morning, she returned to the home where she was boarding, delighted at having found a new sedge—a square-sided marsh grass.

Catherine Furbish was born on May 19, 1834, in Exeter, New Hampshire, the hometown of her mother, Mary Lane Furbish. Her father, Benjamin, was a native of Wells, Maine. When Kate was less than a year old, the family moved to Brunswick, Maine, where they remained. Kate was the eldest and the only girl among five brothers, only three of whom lived past infancy. Her father owned a hardware store in Brunswick. He also manufactured tin and stoves and was something of an inventor, intrigued by new manufacturing and technological devices. At his store he sold mowing machines and wheel rakes, as well as fruit trees and tomato plants he'd raised from seed.

Brunswick was a lively place to grow up, a thriving town of about 4,000 and a business and cultural hub on the Androscoggin River, only a few miles from Merrymeeting Bay and the Atlantic Ocean. Bowdoin College attracted thinkers and doers to Brunswick. The poet Henry Wadsworth Longfellow and its future president, Franklin Pierce, both attended Bowdoin while Kate was growing up. Harriet Beecher Stowe, whose husband taught at the college, wrote *Uncle Tom's Cabin* there. In the years before the Civil War, Brunswick was in fact a center for two important movements: temperance and abolition.

Although Kate soaked up the varied influences around her, the natural world drew her even more strongly. Her father encouraged her interest in nature on long walks around Brunswick. And no doubt she spent hours with her younger brothers, exploring fields and forests. Her father was active in town life, in particular the schools, which were among the best in the state. Kate finished her formal education at a private seminary or girls' high school in

Brunswick. From December 30, 1844, to April 19, 1845, her father paid three dollars for her tuition, with an extra dollar added for Latin. As was true for many women of her time and class, Kate's education was a genteel one—more decorative than useful—and included painting and French literature, both considered appropriate for young women. She even took painting lessons in Paris and Boston.

In 1860, however, when Kate was twenty-eight, her life took a remarkable turn. After attending a series of botany lectures in Boston, given by George L. Goodale, a Maine native and later a professor of botany at Harvard, she was seized by a passion for science. No passing fancy, this was an enduring and serious devotion. After returning to her family's home in Brunswick, she began what would become her life's work: collecting, classifying, and drawing the plants of Maine. Her painting took on new significance, too. Up to that point, although she enjoyed it, it had been a leisure-time hobby, engaged in when more pressing family matters or social events didn't occupy her time; now it became her way of recording her discoveries.

The nineteenth century saw great advances in the natural, observational sciences. Many of these contributions came from amateurs. Nowadays, we think of amateurs as dabblers, not serious scholars, but in the 1800s the word carried its original French meaning: *lovers,* people who do something for the joy of it, not for money or fame. Surely that describes Kate Furbish's interest in plants.

During the Civil War, Kate spent most of her time in Brunswick. She helped the war effort by rolling bandages, but most of her time from late April through October—the growing season in Maine—she walked the countryside nearby, collecting plants and drawing them. The area around Brunswick had a rich diversity of plant habitats: mountains, hills, bogs, shorelines, lakes, forests, and meadows. She explored them all eagerly. In 1862, George

Goodale, the botanist whose lectures had so inspired Kate, finished his survey of all of Maine's known flowering plants. His collection was housed at the Portland Museum of Natural History. This caused great excitement in the plant world since Maine's flora had not been well documented. In 1866, however, the building burned down, destroying all scientific evidence of his work. Perhaps that loss helped to fuel Kate's work in the coming years.

After the war, Kate's life took on a particular rhythm, summer and winter. Although still based at her family's home on O'Brien Street in Brunswick, she in fact spent most of the growing season traveling. County by county, she collected, identified, catalogued, and drew or painted Maine's flowering plants. Most winters she lived in Boston, where she attended lectures, visited family members and botanical colleagues, and fleshed out sketches she made in the field. First she would gather plant specimens and either draw them on the spot or take them home to draw later. Because these plants wilted quickly, she often worked late into the night—after a day spent in the field—capturing the color, the look, the peculiar aspects of each specimen. Many she preserved by drying and pressing. Sometimes she'd dab color onto her sketch while the blossom was at its freshest. Once she'd captured that particular hue, she could go back later and paint in the whole flower. Her medium was water-based paint, the pigment suspended in gum arabic. This made the colors rich and glowing.

Even for her time, Kate was considered small—but only in height, not in force of character. She had a strong profile, square shoulders, and what many observers called a clear-eyed, penetrating gaze. The year 1870 saw all of Kate's strength of character and finely tuned skills reach their zenith. She was thirty-six and living in Brunswick with her aging parents, both of whom were ill, but that spring and summer she was a whirlwind, collecting and painting more specimens than at any other time in her life. She didn't seem bothered by the long hours spent hiking into almost inaccessible places; she didn't complain about mosquitoes, mud, or heat.

By this time, because of the careful attention to detail in her watercolor paintings and tireless field explorations, botany experts were beginning to notice Kate. In fact, she earned the respect of well-known naturalists such as Asa Gray and Sereno Watson. Another naturalist, George Davenport, would become one of two important and lasting professional friends. George was a Boston businessman with a family, and he was passionate about ferns. He and Kate wrote letters, exchanged plant specimens, and helped each other identify unknown samples. Davenport acted as both adviser and mentor for a woman without formal affiliations to any university or botanical society.

The year 1873 was a painful one for Kate. Within a month of each other, both of her parents died. On May 19, she wrote, "At 7:30 A.M. I left the home of my life." Although she'd inherited enough money to live independently, she'd lost her sense of security and family. Only teaching and nursing were open as professions for women of her class and time. Also, the Civil War had killed many men in her generation, so there was no real chance for marriage either. Kate's closeness to cousins on her mother's side helped to ease her grief, and she spent most of that year and into the next visiting family in Delaware.

Early in 1875, with the help of her brother John, who still lived in Brunswick, Kate found a new home. It was on Lincoln Street, in the center of town—nothing grand, just a modest white frame building, but it belonged to her alone. Most of the second floor she turned into a combination of bedroom and studio. Here, day after day, she worked at botanic paintings at her easel in a sunny window. Here also she stored her growing collection of herbarium sheets, with specimens pressed and carefully identified. Kate's Brunswick identity had always been rooted in being a daughter, and then an orphaned daughter. Gradually, however, she came into her own: a mature, independent woman, active in science and art.

In the spring of 1880, Kate was thrilled to at last be traveling in "the Aroostook," Maine's wild northeastern county, home to many unusual plants. While in Orono, outside Bangor, a staging area for her trip, she boarded with the family of Merritt Fernald. Although just a boy, Merritt was already a botanical prodigy. He would go on to work at Harvard's herbarium and eventually teach botany there, and he would become Kate's second lifelong close professional friend.

From Orono, Kate rode the train to Mattawamkeag and then traveled by stage to Fort Fairfield in eastern Aroostook County. She spent two summers in the wilds, gathering plants. Now known for its potato fields, Aroostook was then a vast, largely untouched region of boreal forests, bogs, and lakes on the Canadian border. Two of Kate's plant discoveries bear her name: *Pedicularis furbishiae*, a wild snapdragon, also called wood betony; and *Aster cordifolius* L. var. *furbishiae*. Merritt Fernald himself named the aster for Kate, describing her as a "distinguished artist-botanist . . . who, through her undaunted pluck and faithful brush, has done more than any other to make known the wonderful flora of 'the Garden of Maine.'"

In 1908, after thirty-five years traveling through the state county by county, Kate bequeathed her 1,326 drawings and paintings to Bowdoin College. These were bound into fourteen leather folios, 20 inches by 16½ inches, still on view at the library. Even now, more than a hundred years after she painted them, the watercolors are still vibrant, each plant alive in its own particularities, its own personality. Kate did not think of herself as a decorative artist but rather a "botanic artist," whose mission was to record the special qualities of leaf, flower, stem, twig, fruit, and seed. These illustrations, often combining pencil and watercolor, are remarkable for many reasons: Kate's desire was to capture the essence of the particular specimen she held in her hand, not to draw a generic sample, so petals droop, leaves twist and curl.

Kate was a complex, interesting woman. On the one hand, she'd been brought up to value manners, social convention, and appearances; on the other, her nature seemed much more direct and strong willed, since she burned with the flame of a personal quest. Sometimes, her independent ways put her in conflict with the expectations of the time, and her single-minded pursuit of botany raised some eyebrows, but she persisted. At the age of forty-nine, a year after her solo adventures in Aroostook, she took a grand tour of Europe. In a journal entry from Paris, dated September 16, 1883, she noted her ongoing struggle with the French woman with whom she boarded, who thought that whenever Kate went out exploring, she ought to have a male companion—in this case an elderly French gentleman. "Tis talk, talk, talk, while I want to see, see, see," she wrote, "and I am going to see and think for, and by myself, having proved that a day amounts to more spent alone. I can ask any other Frenchman a question at a proper time as well as he, they all know I am an American, a tourist, and no lounger; and if these gray-hairs and hollow-cheeks are not sufficient to keep me out of harm's way, the more's the pity."

In 1895, Kate helped found the Josselyn Botanical Society of Maine and was its president from 1911 to 1912. Until she was quite old, she attended its annual meetings. Often she left younger members panting behind her as she led excursions into the field. She published articles in the *American Naturalist* and occasionally gave lectures, but the folios were her main focus.

Because of her long and close association with Merritt Fernald, Kate gave her collection of dried plants to the New England Botanical Society. It is now housed at the Gray Herbarium at Harvard and numbers some 4,000 sheets. Kate was quite vigorous until the end of her life, though she often complained of headaches and neuralgia. She spent her last years in Brunswick and Freeport, continuing to collect plant specimens and adding final touches to the folio paintings, which she referred to as "my children." She died of cardiac hypertrophy in 1931, at the age of ninety-seven.

In 1976, Kate Furbish gained unexpected new fame. At the time, the Furbish lousewort was believed to be extinct, but while searching for endangered species in preparation for the building of the Dickey-Lincoln dam and reservoir in Aroostook County, scientists found a number of the wild snapdragons growing along the banks of the St. John River. "Save the Furbish Lousewort" became a rallying cry for environmentalists, concerned about the loss of plant and animal life in that region. Because of the Furbish lousewort, as well as other endangered species, the Dickey-Lincoln hydroelectric project was slowed and then stopped altogether; 88,000 acres of northern Maine wilderness were saved from flooding. This area might serve as a lasting memorial to the woman who dedicated herself to honoring Maine's plant riches, from lowly dandelion to endangered wild snapdragon. But it was Kate Furbish herself who wrote the most fitting description of her own life's work. In a 1909 letter to William DeWitt Hyde, president of Bowdoin College, she summed it up this way:

> I have wandered alone for the most part, on the highways and in the hedges, on foot, in Hayracks, on country mail-stages (often in Aroostook Co., with a revolver on the seat) on improvised rafts, . . . in rowboats, on logs, crawling on hands and knees on the surface of bogs, and backing out, when I dared not walk, in order to procure a coveted treasure. Called 'crazy', a 'Fool'— and this is the way that my work has been done. The Flowers being my only society, and the Manuals the only literature for months together. Happy, happy hours!

ABBIE BURGESS GRANT
(1839–1892)

Lighthouse Keeper

I can depend on you, Abbie!" lighthouse keeper Samuel Burgess called out to his daughter as his dory, *Provider,* headed away from tiny Matinicus Rock. It was January 19, 1856—a dangerous time of year to sail the 25 miles to Rockland, on the mainland, but the family's situation was dire. Usually a government supply cutter dropped off winter supplies in September, but a series of bad storms that fall had prevented any landings. Without more food, the Burgess family would starve. Without more whale oil, the twin light towers would go dark and lives might be lost as ships wrecked on treacherous rocks and shoals.

Abbie stood waving until the dory was just a speck, then she clambered back up the cobblestone beach. Her father had left her in charge, not only of her family but of the lighthouse itself. Although Abbie was only sixteen, she was tall and strong. Her mother, Thankful Burgess, was an invalid, so Abbie was used to cooking, doing housework, and caring for her little sisters, Esther, Lydia, and Mahala. She already knew how to tend the lighthouse lamps. Each evening at sunset, she and her father would climb the narrow spiral stairway to the lamp room, where a circular shelf of

Painting of Abbie Burgess

Argand lamps made a horizontal row. With their hollow wicks, these lamps were especially designed to burn brighter and with less smoke than conventional ones. Still, whale oil created a lot of smoke and a terrible stench when it was heated. Abbie and her father lighted each lamp—there were a total of twenty-eight, fourteen in each light tower. In bad weather, they kept an all-night vigil to make sure the lamps continued to burn. At daybreak, they snuffed the lights, cleaned the glass chimneys, filled the lamps for the following night, and polished the reflectors behind the lamps, which focused and intensified the beams.

When Samuel Burgess sailed for the mainland, the sea was calm, the barometer steady. But soon a terrible nor'easter shook the Rock. Quickly, the temperature dropped below zero. Hurricane-force winds howled so loudly that the family had to shout to be heard, and waves crashed violently against the house. Night after night, Abbie shuttled between the two light towers. Several times she dared to climb out on the catwalk so that she could remove sleet from the windows. One week passed, then another. Thankful and the three younger girls grew more and more frightened when there seemed no relief from the fierce winds, waves, sleet, snow, and rain. Matinicus Rock was practically under water. Huge boulders rolled and shook with each breaker thundering across it. At one point, Abbie dashed outside to rescue her hens from the coop she'd made in the rocks.

The stone house and the light towers stood steadfast, but now water began leaking under the kitchen door. During one particularly savage raging, the original wooden house, which had been her parents' bedroom, tore to pieces and blew into the sea. So much water entered the house that Abbie helped her mother and sisters climb up into one of the lighthouse lamp rooms to ride out the storm.

Four weeks after Samuel Burgess had left Matinicus Rock, ocean swells quieted down enough that he could return home safely, his dory filled with food, whale oil, and medicine for Thankful. Abbie's bravery was noticed by more than just her parents and sisters. Her story was featured in newspapers around the country, praising her efforts to save her family and keep the lights burning. The wives and mothers of seafaring Rockland men created a friendship quilt for Abbie in gratitude for her part in saving countless lives. To honor her faithful service, sea captains whose ships had been warned off the reefs commissioned Revere Silversmiths of Boston to make her a silver bowl. But life went on as usual on Matinicus Rock: isolated, challenging, and—in its own harsh way—beautiful.

Abbie was born in Rockland, Maine, in 1839, the fourth of nine children. Her father worked at a local mill for low wages, and it was a struggle to maintain the big family, especially since Thankful was often bedridden. During Abbie's childhood, Rockland—on Penobscot Bay—was home to a thriving fishing fleet and was a shipbuilding center for the huge, swift sailing vessels called clipper ships. Native Americans had named Rockland "Cutawamkeg," which means "great landing place," and in the 1800s it was a busy seaport. The clipper trade was brisk along the North Atlantic coast, from Boston and Portland to Eastport and on to Halifax, Nova Scotia. Shipping lanes passed close to Matinicus Rock and Matinicus Island, 6 miles away, where a small fishing community lived.

When the position of light keeper at Matinicus Rock came open, Samuel decided to apply. It was a political post, but as long as Democrats stayed in office, he believed he'd be appointed. Although he was over fifty, Samuel seemed eager for this chance to improve his family's fortunes, in spite of the job's insecurity and the confining nature of living on a tiny rock way out at sea. The light keeper's salary was $450 a year, with a quarterly allowance for food and supplies: forty pounds salt pork, fifty-two pounds salt beef, one hundred pounds flour, eighty pounds chip biscuits, eleven-and-a-half pounds brown sugar, six pounds coffee or one-and-a-half pounds tea, five pounds rice, and two gallons dried beans or peas. It was a question of hardship and isolation balanced by the freedom of a fresh start. When the job was offered, Samuel accepted it.

The Burgesses moved to the Rock in the spring of 1853. Abbie was fourteen and probably the most enthusiastic and excited member of the family as the *Provider* set sail, laden with supplies. Only five of the family's nine children were aboard. In addition to Abbie, there were her older brother Benjy, who would be Samuel's assistant, and the three younger girls closest to her age: Esther, Lydia, and Mahala. The two oldest daughters, Miranda and Louisa, mature enough to lead their own lives, remained in Rockland, where they raised the two youngest Burgesses, Rufus and Jane, since the Rock was deemed too dangerous a place for such small children.

Samuel took charge of the lighthouses on the second Tuesday in April. On the mainland, flowers would be blooming soon and trees leafing out, but Matinicus Rock was a barren spot, without even a blade of grass. So many shipwrecks had happened on nearby reefs that President John Quincy Adams commissioned a lighthouse to be built there in 1827. That first winter, during a terrible nor'easter, the lighthouse washed away and was later replaced by twin light towers.

While the Rock itself looked desolate, it was in fact a prime nesting ground for Atlantic puffins, seabirds that never come ashore except to build their nests in shallow depressions in the rocks. Puffins mate for life and always return to the same island to raise their young. During the nesting season, they take on bright, parrot-like colors, which later fade to black and white. When Abbie lived on the Rock, it was home to seventy pairs of nesting puffins, as well as to terns, guillemots, and gulls. The waters surrounding the Rock were rich fishing grounds, full of halibut, flounder, mackerel, and cod.

The lightkeeper's house, in the center of the island, was bigger than the one the Burgesses had rented in Rockland. There was a huge cistern for collecting rainwater, a cobblestone washhouse, a boathouse for *Provider*, and a one-ton bell inside a wooden structure. Matinicus is the third foggiest light station in Maine, with more than 1,700 hours of fog a year. Whenever fog cloaked the island and the lighthouses' beams were dimmed, someone would need to pull the heavy bell rope once every ten or fifteen minutes, round the clock, to warn ships off the reefs.

It became clear early on that Benjy yearned to leave the Rock and join the fishing fleet, but he stayed to assist his father. As well as tending the lights, they built a hundred lobster traps and fished them in stringers in nearby waters. Benjy often sailed back to Rockland for supplies, taking the lobster catch with him to sell on the mainland, a good supplement to his father's salary. It was Abbie's lot to do most of the domestic work at the lighthouse and to watch her younger sisters and brother so her mother could rest. Although she seemed not to complain about this, it was in the light towers where she truly felt happiest.

Since Benjy was often away, Abbie became her father's helper, showing both aptitude and keen interest from the beginning. For Abbie's mother and sisters, life on the Rock often felt confining, boring, and lonely. They talked about what they'd left behind, what they couldn't do anymore, what they didn't have: schools, libraries, parties, gardens, friends outside the family. To Abbie, however, the island offered beautiful vistas and a vast round world of sea and sky, endlessly fascinating and changeable. Eagerly, she learned how to tend the lights. No one expected a girl to do this, but Abbie had found what she loved, and she convinced her father that she was up to the task.

Soon enough, Benjy left the Rock to join a mother ship with twelve fishing dories, which sailed for Bay Chaleur, just below the Gaspé Peninsula in Quebec, Canada. Before Samuel gave his permission, however, Benjy and Abbie had to persuade him that she could handle the job of assistant keeper. Finally, Samuel relented, and Abbie took on her life's work. Not only was she strong, well-trained, and responsible enough to serve as assistant keeper, but she also helped her father lobster, then haul up the dory by hand— dressed in oilskins over her long skirts.

Part of the light keeper's job was to write in a log each day, recording weather conditions and anything remarkable that happened. During her watch in the light towers, Abbie read these logs avidly. In an entry dated June 11, 1833, one keeper had measured Matinicus Rock and "found it according to his figures 2,350 feet long, 567 feet wide, 34⁹⁄₁₀ acres." In January, 1839, breakers over 40 feet high had carried away the keeper's house, though he and his family had escaped in a dory and were later picked up by a passing schooner.

Within a few months, Samuel Burgess trusted Abbie enough that he would sail to Rockland, alone, every Monday to sell lobsters and buy supplies. He'd stay overnight and sail back the next day, which meant that Abbie was in charge of tending all the lights in his absence.

In March of 1856, officials from the Lighthouse Board visited the Rock to plan for improvements to the lights. By now, clipper ship traffic was waning. It was only a matter of time before steamships, though still expensive to run, would supplant the giant sailing ships. The Burgesses had always believed the lights shone as far as 15 miles out to sea, but it turned out the distance was closer to nine. Plans included building a second light tower and installing Fresnel lenses to replace the old Argand ones. Now, both lighthouses would shine with brighter, more piercing beams.

In May, Abbie's brother Benjy returned to the Rock. With the decline of the clipper trade and subsequent job losses in Rockland, employment on fishing boats declined as well. Although her brother could now help their father again, it was Abbie who still lighted the lamps at night. In June, a crew installed an engine for a steam-driven fog whistle. Instead of manually ringing the bell, the Burgesses just needed to keep a fire burning under a boiler so the whistle would blow.

During that winter, stores of food and whale oil again ran very low because bad weather had prevented the supply cutter from visiting the Rock. In fact, Samuel believed his family would starve to death in just a few weeks if he didn't reprovision immediately. In spite of bad weather, he headed to Rockland, alone. When Samuel did not return, Benjy built a dory and sailed off to look for his father, as well as to get more food and whale oil. Once again, Abbie was responsible not only for her family's welfare but for the safety of mariners out at sea. A week passed. Benjy still hadn't returned nor had Samuel. The flour barrel was empty, and there were no more dried apples and raisins. Abbie rationed her mother and sisters to an egg a day, plus one cup of cornmeal mush.

At last, in March, her father and brother returned safely. A month later, construction began on new twin towers, 180 feet apart. One was 10 feet from the house; the other was 140 feet away. This meant more work for the lightkeeper, though a covered walkway was also created between the two towers. Brighter lamps were installed. A 24-foot by 26-foot frame house was built as the future home for an assistant lightkeeper. Samuel and Thankful moved into it, while the children continued to live in the original house.

Three years later, Lydia was seventeen and wanted to go to Boston to attend art school. Esther was sixteen and Mahala fifteen; both were eager to leave the island for a broader life. Thankful, too, was tired of living on the Rock. But Samuel and Abbie did not want to go. The 1860 election sealed the family's future: When the Republican candidate, Abraham Lincoln, was elected president, Democratically-affiliated Samuel Burgess lost his job. On a trip to Rockland after the elections, Samuel urged his friend Captain John Grant to apply for the position. In turn, Grant was appointed lightkeeper to begin in March of 1861.

Twenty-two-year-old Abbie felt so sad at the thought of leaving the light station that her father allowed her to stay on to help the new family learn the ropes. The Grants, including three sons, were large, friendly, and robust. The mother was as vigorous as the others and enjoyed Abbie's company. The youngest son, Isaac, took great interest in the running of the lighthouses. Soon he was also very interested in Abbie herself. The two fell in love and were married the next summer. For fourteen years they stayed on the Rock, serving as paid assistants to John Grant. Abbie and Isaac's four children—Francis, Malvina, Mary, and Harris—were born on Matinicus Rock. Another child, two-year-old Bessie, died suddenly and was buried there because the weather was too severe to leave the island.

In 1875, after twenty-two years of service at the light station, Abbie moved off Matinicus Rock when Isaac was appointed keeper of Whitehead Light Station, also in Maine. She served as his paid assistant until they both retired in 1890. In her final letter to a friend, Abbie wrote:

> Sometimes I think the time is not far distant when I shall climb these litehouse stairs no more. It has almost seemed to me that the lite was part of myself. Many nights I have watched my part of the night and then could not sleep the rest of the night, thinking nervously what might happen should the lite fail. . . . In all these years I always put the lamps in order in the morning and

I lit them at sunset. Those old lamps on Matinicus Rock—I often dream of them. When I dream of them, it always seems to me that I have been away a long while, and I am hurrying toward the Rock to lite the lamps there before sunset. I feel a great deal more worried in my dreams than when I am awake.

I wonder if the care of the litehouse will follow my soul after it has left this worn-out body! If I ever have a gravestone, I would like it in the form of a lighthouse, or beacon.

Abbie Burgess Grant died in 1892 at the age of fifty-three and was buried in Forest Hill Cemetery in South Thomaston, near Spruce Head and the Whitehead Light Station. In 1945, historian Edward Rowe Snow, who had read Abbie's letter, commissioned a miniature lighthouse to be built—an aluminum scale replica of the one on Matinicus Rock. This he placed on top of her grave: a fitting honor for a woman who, defying the conventions of the time, spent her life lighting beacons along the rocky Maine coast.

Keepers no longer tend the lights on Matinicus Rock; the lights have been automated since 1984 and are maintained by the Coast Guard. Thanks to the National Audubon Society's Puffin Project, the seabirds Abbie so enjoyed watching—once hunted to near extinction for their colorful plumage—have returned to nest on her beloved Rock.

LILLIAN M. N. STEVENS

(1844–1914)

Temperance Activist and Social Reformer

*L*illian Stevens wasn't afraid of anything or anyone. You might not share her views on a particular issue, but you'd much rather have her fighting on your side than against you. More than one man came to find this out too late. It was midmorning, so one story goes, when Lillian appeared in the office of an elected official. As part of his duties, he was supposed to enforce "Maine's law," the statewide prohibition on manufacturing and selling alcohol, originally enacted in 1851. In fact, she knew him to be a slacker.

Lillian had a ship-of-state bearing, imposing and confident in her long black Victorian dress and bonnet. Although many of Portland's homeless women and children knew Lillian for her kindness, on this particular day her looks and manner were severe. She got right to the point: If re-elected, she asked the man, would he start cracking down on the liquor traffic?

The fellow tipped his hat back to get a better look at her. Then he propped his feet up on his desk, picked up an orange, and

Lillian M. N. Stevens

cut it in half. Mrs. Stevens was one of those temperance ladies—
he knew the type—always waving Bibles and praying for sinners,
while demolishing barrels of whiskey with their sharp little hatch-
ets. They'd already stirred up trouble, but you didn't need to take
them too seriously. Without saying a word, the man slowly ate one
of his orange halves. When he finished, he deigned to tell Mrs.
Stevens that what he did was none of her business.

Lillian's long skirts hissed as she turned to leave his office. "I
shall make it my business," she told him, "to do all I can to defeat
you." The time would come when he'd be sorry he didn't remove his
hat, take his feet off his desk, and ask if she'd like the other half
of that orange, she added.

That morning the official may have smirked, but Lillian kept
her word: She labored mightily to defeat his re-election bid. After
his loss at the polls, he at least had the good grace to apologize for
his rudeness—and for his unwillingness to share his orange.

While the details of this story may have been embellished
over the years, it was typical of Lillian to stand her ground. From
a young age, she was not only aware of social causes but willing to
put her beliefs on the line, starting with the presidential campaign
of 1856, when she was only twelve. At issue was the abolition of
slavery.

Because John C. Frémont, the pro-abolition candidate, was
very popular in her hometown of Dover, Maine, Lillian saw a great
many flags emblazoned with his name as she walked to school each
day. She felt so passionately about the abolitionist cause that she
sewed her own banner and stitched Frémont's name across it. To
publicize her support, she stretched the banner across the road in
front of her house, tying it between two tall pine trees. One day an
old man, who was driving his horse and wagon into town, passed
under Lillian's banner. Apparently he hated the idea of abolition so
much that he pulled over, left his wagon, and started climbing one

of the pines to cut the flag down. Lillian, watching from a window, quickly figured out what the man was doing. She dashed outside toward the wagon and startled his horse enough to make it bound away. The man scrambled down the tree trunk and chased after his horse and wagon, leaving the John C. Frémont banner undisturbed.

Lillian Marilla Nickerson Ames was born March 1, 1844, at the family farmhouse on the edge of the little central-Maine town of Dover (now Dover-Foxcroft). Her mother was Nancy Fowler Ames; her father, Nathaniel Ames, was a teacher. Hers was a happy childhood, spent studying at the village school and playing in nearby hills and woods with her brother and two sisters. When she was twelve, however—the same year she made the banner for the anti-slavery candidate—her older brother died. This loss turned her thoughts to religion and to caring for others.

Lillian was a slender girl with black hair and hazel-colored eyes. Her voice was low, her face composed and serious. She was an eager student who loved school. After she graduated from Foxcroft Academy in the town next door, she studied at Westbrook Seminary (now part of the University of New England) in the suburbs of Portland, Maine. Even then, Lillian impressed teachers and fellow students with her quiet authority. In *Lillian M. N. Stevens: A Life Sketch*, Lillian's daughter, Gertrude Stevens Leavitt, relates this story:

> Once when a young woman said she was sorry for her [Lillian] because she cared more for books than bonnets, and solid study rather than social success, a classmate replied: "No one need be sorry for Lillian Ames. She will be remembered years after the rest of us are dead and forgotten. I cannot tell just why I think so, but I am perfectly sure that she will make good."

Lillian's next venture was teaching at both the Spruce Street and Stroudwater schools in Westbrook. Although teaching was one of few professions open to women at the time, traditionally only men were hired for the winter term. Many almost-grown boys, who worked on farms or on boats during the spring, summer, and fall, attended school in the winter and were thought too big and rough for women to handle. But not too big and rough for Lillian. As one of the first women hired to teach during the winter term, she defied convention and did it handily. She was a strict, demanding teacher, and a popular one. Not only did her students learn, they liked and respected her.

In 1865, when Michael Stevens, a well-to-do salt and grain wholesaler, asked Lillian to marry him, she accepted. In that era, because married women were not allowed to teach, Lillian's decision meant the end of her teaching career. For a woman of her energy, intelligence, and need to be useful, this choice must have been a difficult one. Nevertheless, she threw herself into the role of Victorian wife, becoming a fine cook, hostess, and seamstress. She and Michael moved into his family's large brick house—built in 1803 by his father—in Stroudwater, a historic section of Portland. (The house remains in the family, now occupied by the Stevens' great-great-grandson.)

Lillian and Michael had one daughter, whom they named Gertrude Rose. Soon though, the wider world beyond the domestic sphere called to Lillian, and she responded. In the winter of 1873–1874, news of the "Women's Temperance Crusade" stirred her activist nature. During that campaign, female churchgoers marched into Ohio saloons—or knelt outside them in the snow—to sing hymns and pray. Similar demonstrations swept the country, closing thousands of saloons in twenty-three states. Although most soon reopened, the temperance cause ignited a wildfire.

Anti-alcohol groups had been agitating since the early part of the nineteenth century, but they were small and not centrally organized. Now, however, women began to unite. In November, 1874, the Woman's Christian Temperance Union (WCTU) was founded in Cleveland, Ohio.

In spite of her own settled, privileged life, Lillian was very aware of problems affecting poor women and children. She believed, as did growing numbers of other women—and some men—that alcoholism was at the root of society's major troubles, poverty and domestic violence among them. Before the Civil War, some Northern white women had worked hard for abolition; now, after African-American men gained the right to vote in 1870, many of these same women turned their attention to temperance and suffrage.

During the summer of 1875, Lillian took young Gertrude to Old Orchard Beach on the Atlantic Ocean 20 miles south of Portland. Crowded into an open-air tent, they heard a speech by Frances E. Willard, a well-known educator and temperance activist. Lillian listened, spellbound, to Frances's words. Here, Lillian felt, was her calling. After the meeting, she rushed to the stage and introduced herself. The two would become close lifelong friends and colleagues.

Although Maine's prohibition law had been in effect in one form or another since 1851—due in large part to the efforts of Portland's mayor, Neal Dow—liquor could still be found. That fall, inspired by Frances Willard, Lillian organized the state's first Woman's Christian Temperance group, the Stroudwater Union, and became its first president. In 1878, she was elected Maine's president of the WCTU, an office she held for the rest of her life.

Lillian's husband, Michael Stevens, shared her temperance zeal and was very supportive of her reform efforts. To make it easier for Lillian to focus on her work, they hired a governess to care for Gertrude. As president of Maine's WCTU, Lillian visited almost every town in the state, driving her beloved horse, Madge, some 50,000 miles. For most women, belonging to the WCTU was their first experience with flexing political muscle. Lillian's example—her sense of herself as a strong and confident woman, her clarity of purpose, her willingness to stand up for what she thought was right—made her a galvanizing force, a role model, not only in Maine but around the country. Women flocked to her side.

In 1879, Frances Willard ran for president of the National WCTU, whose offices were in Chicago. Her platform embraced woman's suffrage as a way to promote temperance. This double-pronged activism split the organization into two warring factions. Lillian stood by her friend, who won the election. Under Willard's leadership, "Do Everything" became the WCTU's rallying cry, as different local chapters fought for different causes, among them: suffrage, labor laws, and prison reform—all under the umbrella of temperance. At the WCTU National Convention in 1880, Lillian was chosen to serve as assistant recording secretary. She rose quickly in the ranks. By 1894, she'd become vice-president-at-large. As Frances Willard's right-hand woman, she now traveled the country fighting the powerful liquor industry, as well as advocating for social reforms of many kinds. By 1895, the WCTU had approximately 135,000 members, making it the largest organization of American women at that time. As such, it had an early and profound influence on women's advancement toward political power.

In 1896, after the Turkish massacre of Christian Armenians, refugees from the fighting fled to France, where Frances Willard, visiting England on temperance business, heard about their plight. She sent telegrams, begging each WCTU leader to help twenty-five refugees resettle in her community. Immediately Lillian answered, saying Portland would open its doors to fifty Armenians. She met them at the docks in Portland; they'd been told to look for a woman with a white ribbon on her coat, a WCTU symbol. Lillian and other Maine union members gathered clothing and food and found housing and jobs. Some refugees may even have camped in her backyard. The first child born to Portland's Armenian community was named Willard Stevens.

While Lillian thrived as a national-level temperance leader, she also kept an eye on social problems closer to home. Her friend Frances Willard wrote that "the streets of Portland, Maine, have not a sight more familiar and surely none more welcome to all save evil-doers than Mrs. Stevens in her phaeton [carriage] rapidly driving her spirited horse from police station to Friendly Inn, from Erring Women's Refuge to the sheriff's office." She prodded her wealthy friends to be generous with their time and resources, and she led by example. Within a fifteen-year span, a total of nineteen homeless children lived at the Stevens' house on Westbrook Street. Lillian spearheaded the drive to create an Industrial School for Girls and was a founder of the Temporary Home for Women and Children, where she spent many hours volunteering. She also served as treasurer and then president of the National Council of Women, a group that advanced women's work in education, reform, and philanthropy.

After Frances Willard's death in February, 1898, Lillian became her handpicked successor as president of the National WCTU. Two years later, Lillian also became vice-president of the World WCTU. As such, she organized international conventions in Boston, Brooklyn, Scotland, and Switzerland. The scope of these endeavors was breathtaking, the pace dizzying. In 1905, for example, Lillian and her assistant, Anna Gordon, traveled 10,000 miles in just nine weeks on temperance business.

During Lillian's tenure as president of the National WCTU, she grappled with many thorny issues, including friction with the National Woman's Suffrage Association. Lillian herself was a passionate supporter of women's right to vote. Even so, the NWSA asked her to stop promoting its cause. Its leaders felt that the future of woman's suffrage was being jeopardized by its association with temperance and prohibition, since the WCTU had powerful enemies in both the liquor industry and in politics. It was a painful schism. Reluctantly, Lillian agreed to withdraw from the Maine Suffrage Association.

Still, under Lillian's direction, the National Woman's Christian Temperance Union acted on more than just the anti-liquor front. For example, it lobbied strongly on behalf of the Pure Food and Drug Act, which passed in 1906, and the Mann Act of 1910. The Mann Act outlawed the transportation of women and girls between states and out of the country for "immoral purposes." In her 1910 address to the National Convention of the WCTU, Lillian noted that "buying, selling, deceiving, forcing and imprisoning their victims are among the methods employed by the trade, and the terrible evil is widespread."

For her time, Lillian Stevens was an interesting crucible of unusual qualities. A product of the Victorian era, she was ladylike, a genial hostess with impeccable manners. She could also wither those who opposed her. To a twenty-first century reader, her language of "sin" and "evildoers" may sound overbearing or moralistic, even patronizing. Undoubtedly some members of the WCTU did look down their noses at "sinners," but Lillian herself seems to have genuinely loved her fellow human beings and worked for social change. She combined her deep religious faith with commonsense practicality about how to best aid those in need. Workers at the WCTU's national headquarters in Evanston, Illinois, looked forward to her visits. Not only did they appreciate her clear, logical mind and forceful direction, they also loved her wit, her friendliness, and the excitement she brought to their cause. They fondly called her "the chieftain."

In 1911, Maine's prohibition law was challenged in a referendum vote. Lillian organized a statewide campaign in support of keeping the ban against liquor sales. When the measure narrowly passed, keeping prohibition, Lillian felt that finally the time was right to push for a national Prohibition Amendment to the Constitution. Letter-writing campaigns, fasting, prayer vigils, public speeches, parades, street meetings, rallies—all culminated in a National Constitutional Prohibition Amendment Day on January 15, 1914. That morning, Lillian attended a gathering at the First Free Baptist Church of Portland, where she gave her last speech. She ended by saying:

> Some glad day the states in which today is entrenched the liquor system will rejoice that it has been abolished. Science, philanthropy, reform, religion, and the business world are testifying against the liquor traffic. In the light of all this we can see prohibition looming up all the way from Mt. Kineo in the east to Mt. Shasta in the west, from the pine forests in the north to the palmetto groves in the south. We verily believe that the amendment for National Constitutional Prohibition is destined to prevail and that by 1920 the United States flag will float over a nation redeemed from the home-destroying, heart-breaking curse of the liquor traffic.

Lillian did not live to see the Prohibition Amendment to the Constitution pass Congress and be ratified by forty-four states in 1919, but she had helped to lay the groundwork. While the Prohibition experiment, repealed in 1933, proved unsuccessful, her work on behalf of social justice endured.

On April 6, 1914, at the age of seventy, Lillian died of kidney failure at home, in the company of her husband, her daughter

Gertrude, and her good friend and successor as president of the WCTU, Anna Gordon. Her last words were, "My full day's work is done." Gertrude nodded, then said, "And well done."

Lillian chose to be cremated and was buried in the old Stroudwater Cemetery across the street from her house. After her death, flags in Maine flew at half-mast, the first time a woman was so honored. Tributes poured in from around the world. In her memory, the WCTU presented a water fountain to the City of Portland in 1917: a bronze statue of a young girl, set on a Maine granite base. There was also a drinking trough for horses and a special basin for dogs and birds. This fountain now stands inside the courtyard of the Portland Public Library's main branch on Congress Street.

After her mother's death, Gertrude delivered this quiet appreciation: "Mother had a cheerful smile, was a loyal friend, and most unselfish. She often said 'to love one's self last went a long way towards establishing the kingdom of Heaven in one's heart.' She demonstrated that so well. She was utterly fearless. She saw all sides of a question. She didn't talk about her religion but lived it every day of her life."

SARAH ORNE JEWETT
(1849–1909)

Writer from the Country
of the Pointed Firs

*I*t was a fine June morning. Cardinals shrilled from the branches of willows along the riverbank—a bead of sound, a flash of red. Nine-year-old Sarah Jewett closed her eyes a moment to savor the sweet smell of lilacs while her father's horse and buggy swayed along the packed dirt tracks of a country road. But just as quickly her eyes popped open; she didn't want to miss a thing. Her father, a country doctor, had invited her to forego school for the day and make house calls with him, and she had jumped at the chance. Now they sat, side by side, on the seat of his buggy. Sunlight sheened off the horse's rump and warmed Sarah's dark hair.

Suddenly, Dr. Jewett reined in his horse, climbed down from the buggy, and motioned for Sarah to follow. Out of the mass of vines and tangled greenery beside the lane, he pointed to a particular shrub with twisted twigs, splayed out in all directions—witch hazel. She remembered the surprise of its feathery yellow flowers last fall, how they'd bloomed only after the leaves died back, on the coattails of a snowstorm.

Sarah Orne Jewett (right) with her friend, Emily Tyson, 1905

Later, when they stopped at a weather-beaten farmhouse, she followed her father inside and observed everything that happened; she listened to him draw his elderly patient into conversation, noticed which herbs and medicines he prescribed. Not only did she learn about healing during these trips, she also soaked up landscape and seascape, characters and stories—and the intricate workings of human nature.

Years later, when she'd become a well-known writer, Sarah told an interviewer, "The best of my education was received in my father's buggy and the places to which he carried me." She credited him with encouraging her to feel sympathy "for the dreams of others" and with calling "my attention to trees, birds and flowers. He urged me to tell things just as they are, and said nothing in the world is uninteresting if you only look at it long enough. In this way he taught me how to write."

Theodora Sarah Orne Jewett was born in South Berwick, Maine, on September 3, 1849, to Caroline F. Perry and Dr. Theodore H. Jewett. The middle child, she had one older sister, Mary, born in 1847, and another sister six years younger, Caroline, nicknamed Carrie. South Berwick was a small port, 10 miles up the Piscataqua River from the Atlantic, in the most southerly corner of Maine. When Sarah was little, her family lived in the center of town, in a big white house belonging to her paternal grandfather; later they moved to a smaller house next door. Her grandfather had run off to sea as a boy and worked his way up to captain, then shipbuilder and wealthy merchant. Sarah's maternal grandfather was a well-to-do doctor, with whom her father had interned.

By all accounts, Sarah's formal education was erratic. She attended a "dame school" but sometimes skipped classes, suffering, she claimed, from "instant drooping if ever I were shut up in school." She also missed days because of poor health—bouts of rheumatoid arthritis—for which her father recommended lots of outdoor exercise. "I wasn't like the usual village schoolgirl," she once wrote. "I grew up as naturally as a plant grows, not having been clipped back or forced in any unnatural direction." Free to roam the town, she loved listening to old sailors' stories at the docks and the latest gossip from customers at the dry goods store. Despite spells with painful swollen joints, she became an expert horsewoman. She also learned to sail and row on the river; in winter she skated, snowshoed, and sledded with her sisters. "Wild and shy" were the words she used to describe her childhood self, yet her mother also taught her to entertain and to manage a household.

Both of Sarah's parents encouraged her to read, and she did so avidly, ranging widely in her family's library. As a girl, she wrote poetry and kept detailed journals. In her early teens, she read Harriet Beecher Stowe's novel, *The Pearl of Orr's Island*, which dealt with everyday characters on a real Maine island. The rural people and places she'd come to love, she realized, were worthy subjects for literature.

In 1866, Sarah graduated from Berwick Academy, the oldest preparatory school in the state. She thought about studying medicine, but because her health wasn't robust enough she abandoned that idea. While continuing to live with her family, she often visited relatives in Boston for parties, plays, and concerts. And always, she wrote. When just nineteen, she published her first work of fiction, a melodramatic romance entitled "Jenny Garrow's Lovers." It appeared in the magazine *The Flag of Our Union* under a pseudonym, A. C. Eliot. Another story, "Mr. Bruce," was published in the December 1869 issue of the *Atlantic Monthly*, also under a pseudonym. At her sister Mary's urging, she told the rest of her family that she was the author, though at first she regretted doing this because now the story "no longer belonged *all to me*."

By 1873, when she was twenty-four, Sarah was actively seeking advice from editors about how to improve her writing, in particular William Dean Howells, a well-known writer and the editor of the *Atlantic Monthly*. As much as she sought out suggestions for mastering her craft, she also had a sturdy, independent sense of her own writer's path, regardless of editors' literary taste. Artistic independence was easier for her, of course, than for some other women writers of her time since, as the daughter of an upper-middle-class family, she never had to make a living from her work and could focus on it exclusively without financial worries.

Sarah was drawn to write what she called "sketches" of country life. These emphasized creating characters rather than showcasing plots. Her aesthetic, "imaginative realism," drew from the local color movement of regional fiction but also from such writers as French novelist Gustave Flaubert, whose fiction, rooted in commonplace details, she greatly admired. Sarah was so impressed with his work that she pinned two of his quotations to her desk: "Write ordinary life as if writing history," and "The writer's job is to make one dream."

In 1877, at the urging of William Dean Howells, Sarah collected her stories about small-town life into her first book, *Deephaven*. It sold well and, in general, was reviewed enthusiastically. With her first royalties, Sarah bought a chestnut thoroughbred. "I believe I should not like Sheila half so well if she were tamer and entirely reliable," she wrote of her horse—in some ways a mirror of herself. "I glory in her good spirits and think she has a right to be proud and willful if she chooses."

By the late 1870s, Sarah was publishing stories in such magazines as *Harper's Monthly* and *Scribner's*, as well as the *Atlantic Monthly*. While she wrote about the disappearing virtues of Maine farms and coastal villages, she was also becoming part of a worldly artistic community. Her publisher, James T. Fields, and his wife, Annie Adams Fields, became her close friends. Annie was a writer, a social reformer, and a generous hostess. The Fields lived at 148 Charles Street, at the foot of Boston's Beacon Hill, in a large mansion, which they opened to new and established writers of the day. At dinner parties and readings—often lasting late into the night—the Fields created a fertile atmosphere where Sarah shared her work and ideas with such famous authors as Longfellow, Emerson, Whittier, and Hawthorne. She also came to know Matthew Arnold, Henry James, and Charles Dickens when they happened to visit Boston.

But at the heart of Sarah's fiction, as in her life, lay friendships between women, whom she portrayed as self-reliant, independent, and in charge of their own lives. Whether widowed or unmarried, these characters created a place for themselves in a world where women's futures were usually defined by marriage and motherhood. Early in her career, Sarah established a network of powerful women friends, like fellow-writers Celia Thaxter and Amy Lowell, who also frequented the Fields' get-togethers.

When John Greenleaf Whittier once asked Sarah why she'd never married, she supposedly answered that she had "more need of a wife" than a husband. "I do not wish to be married," she wrote on another occasion. "Would you have me bury the talent God has given me? Doing this work lovingly and well is the best way I can see of making myself useful in the world." In the companion book to the film biography of Sarah Orne Jewett, *Master Smart Woman*, Cynthia Keyworth notes that Sarah was "more of a bachelor than a spinster," emphasizing the fullness and exuberance of her chosen lifestyle, her freedom from the usual constraints imposed on Victorian women.

In September, 1878, Sarah's father died—her earliest dear friend and teacher. During her grieving time, she found the friendship of Annie Fields especially comforting. Less than three years later, in 1881, Annie's husband, James, also died. In the summer of 1882, the two women sailed to Europe, drawn together by their shared loss, and during that trip, they fell in love. They became life partners and champions of each other's work, as well as travel companions. In that era, such intimate, intense, and supportive relationships between two women were called "Boston marriages." Sarah and Annie were widely accepted as a couple. For the next two decades, Sarah's life took on a seasonal pattern: She spent half a year at 148 Charles Street and half a year at her family's home in South Berwick or at Annie's summer house in Manchester-by-the-Sea, Massachusetts.

When apart, the two exchanged frequent letters. Not only did they express their feelings—using many endearments and the pet names "Pinny" for Sarah and "Fuffy" for Annie—but they recorded the details of their lives and their work. In 1883, after William Dean Howells declined to publish Sarah's short story, "A White Heron," she wrote to Annie:

> Dear Fuff,
> . . . but what shall I do with my white heron now she is written? She isn't a very good magazine story but I love her. I mean to keep her for the beginning of my next book.

"A White Heron," now one of Sarah's best-known and most anthologized stories—and an example of early environmental awareness—deals with an unsophisticated country girl named Sylvie, who chooses to protect the hiding place of a beautiful, rare heron rather than expose it to a young man from the city who wants to kill it and stuff it to add to his trophy collection.

In her novel, *A Country Doctor*, published in 1884, Sarah tried to capture something of her father's character in Dr. Leslie, a kind and intelligent man who adopts a child, Nan Prince. Echoing her own childhood adventures with her father, Sarah has Nan accompany Dr. Leslie as he makes house calls on his rural patients. Nan, who runs wild in the woods, as did Sarah, decides to become a doctor herself and in the end gives up the idea of marriage and children so that she can achieve her dream. Of all Sarah's works, this was her favorite.

During the 1890s, Sarah continued to write in spite of many personal sorrows. Her mother died in 1891, as did her brother-in-law a year later. In 1894 it was her very close friend Celia Thaxter who died. Then in 1897, her younger sister Carrie passed away, leaving behind a son, Theodore Eastman, to whom Sarah was devoted.

From January to September of 1896, when she was forty-nine, Sarah's novel, *The Country of the Pointed Firs*, was serialized in the *Atlantic Monthly*. In November it appeared in book form. This loosely structured novel of linked stories was narrated by a woman writer from the city who spends a summer in Dunnet's Landing, a place much like the St. George Peninsula on the Maine coast which Sarah and Annie had visited the previous year. Still considered a masterpiece, *The Country of the Pointed Firs* was both a critical and a commercial success, and Sarah became one of America's most popular and respected writers. The narrator is deeply changed by her encounters with the residents of the town and outlying islands, yet she keeps herself out of the way as the stories of local lives unfold. The book is full of humor, compassion, and keen insight, and its style is carefully crafted. In describing the odd character of Joanna, a woman who lives alone on an island as penance for a tragic love affair, Sarah's narrator muses, "In the life of each of us, . . . there is a place remote and islanded, and given to endless regret or secret happiness."

Sarah's 1901 book, *The Tory Lover*, a historical novel set at the Hamilton House in South Berwick, tried to portray a passionate love affair between a man and a woman. But it was much less convincing than her earlier work. After reading the novel, Henry James wrote:

> Go back to the dear Country of the Pointed Firs, come back to the palpable present intimate that throbs

responsive, and that wants, misses, needs you, God knows, and suffers woefully in your absence.

During that same year, Sarah became the first woman to receive an honorary degree from Bowdoin College. This honor celebrated a writing career that spanned more than thirty years and produced over 170 works of fiction. In September of 1902, on her fifty-third birthday, Sarah was thrown from a carriage, injuring her spine so badly that she never fully recovered. In December of that year, still recuperating in South Berwick, she wrote to Annie Fields:

> My darling, you know that it goes very hard with me that I can't be with you on Christmas. We are closer than ever in love and friendship and belongingness, aren't we? It is wonderful with all the chances and changes of life that I have managed to have part of Christmas Day in Charles Street for twenty years without a break.

Although dizziness and terrible headaches hindered Sarah from writing fiction, she was able in her remaining years to help younger women writers, such as Mary Ellen Chase and Edith Wharton. Most significantly, she mentored Willa Cather, whom she met at Annie Fields' house in 1905. Struggling as a journalist in New York City, Willa turned to Sarah for advice and encouragement. Sarah urged her to return to Nebraska, where she'd grown up, so that she could focus on the kind of material she was driven to write. In a 1908 letter to her young protégée, Sarah, who'd always thought of her own work as "experimental," advised this: "Don't try to write the kind of short story that this or that magazine wants—write the truth, and let them take it or leave it. . . . Make a way of your own. If that way happens to be new, don't let that frighten you." Inspired by Jewett's example and belief in her talent, Willa Cather did return to Nebraska, creating such memorable novels as *O Pioneers!*, *My Ántonia*, and *The Song of the Lark*, set in the prairie landscape she knew and loved.

In March of 1909, while staying with Annie Fields in Boston, Sarah had a stroke which left her partially paralyzed. At the end of April, she returned to South Berwick, where she convalesced in her beloved old white house on the town square. "I was born here and I hope to die here leaving the lilac bushes still green, all the chairs in place," she wrote. Her wish came true. After a second stroke, she died at home on June 24, 1909, just after the lilacs bloomed. She was fifty-nine.

In 1910, Sarah's friends established the Sarah Orne Jewett Scholarship Fund at Simmons College. It honored her women-centered stories and the great potential she saw in expanding young women's horizons. In 1911, Annie Fields published a book of her and Sarah's letters, though her publisher insisted that she delete many of the endearments and expressions of affection, believing that society might "misinterpret" their friendship.

During the first half of the twentieth century, Sarah Orne Jewett's writing, often dismissed as "minor," was relegated to the local-color shelf, read by devotees of Maine's rural past. But in recent decades, feminist scholars have re-examined her books in a new light. In *Sarah Orne Jewett: Her World and Her Work*, critic Paula Blanchard describes her as "an unsurpassed chronicler and interpreter of women's lives."

Sarah's family home in South Berwick, maintained just as she left it, is owned by the Society for the Preservation of New England Antiquities, as is the Hamilton House, described in *The Tory Lover*. Both are open to the public.

Sarah Orne Jewett's real legacy, of course, remains her body of literary work. It is important that we remain connected to the past, she reminds us, that we treasure simple pleasures and the unspoiled bounty of nature. Sarah herself described it this way: "I fear this world is on the point of vanishing. But what a luminous beauty its sense of decay gives off!"

It's not just a long-ago world she sought to animate, however. Even today, her characters inspire readers to follow where their deepest natures lead them. "I long to impress upon every boy and girl this truth: that it is not one's surroundings that can help or hinder. . . . it is having a growing purpose in one's life to make the most of whatever is in one's reach."

CORNELIA "FLY ROD" CROSBY
(1854–1946)

Sportswoman & Journalist
of the Maine Woods

On March 16, 1896, the Second Annual Sportsmen's Exposition opened at Madison Square Garden in New York City. Front and center at Maine's exhibit was Cornelia "Fly Rod" Crosby—noted fisherwoman, hunter, sports journalist, and enthusiastic promoter of wilderness tourism in her home state. "Camp Maine," as it was called, took up six exhibitors' spaces. It included a cabin of peeled logs—studded with stuffed deer heads—and fish tanks full of a hundred live Maine salmon and trout. Fly Rod demonstrated fly-fishing and extolled Maine's virtues to all passersby. She wore a special Paris-inspired hunting costume designed for her by Spaulding Brothers of New York: a suit of tanned green leather, with a mid calf skirt, matching tall green lace-up boots, and a tailored jacket, worn with a red sweater and jaunty red-and-green hat. The newspapers of the day praised Fly Rod and her daring outfit, but years later she would tell an interviewer that many women were scandalized:

Cornelia "Fly Rod" Crosby

Yes, sir, Fly Rod with her wild and wooly guides, her speaking acquaintance with the beasts and birds of the great north country, was looked upon as some aborigine! I think many were disappointed because I did not emit a warwhoop every so often. What the men thought, I can't say, but I am positive the women all regarded me as a first-class freak!

More than 8,000 people each day stopped at "Camp Maine" during the exposition's six-day run. As exciting as the fish tanks, the log cabin, and lifelike taxidermy turned out to be, it was forty-two-year-old Fly Rod who proved the biggest draw. By 1896, she was a celebrity, the "Queen of Anglers." *The New York Journal* described her as "an athletic country girl, born in the state of Maine . . . as proud of her $1,000 collection of fishing tackle as most girls are of souvenir spoons or blue and white china." The Sportsmen's Exposition of 1896 was important to Fly Rod for another reason: During that short week, she made a lifelong friend, Annie Oakley, who was appearing at the exposition as a sharpshooter.

Cornelia's parents, Lemuel Crosby and Thurza Cottle Porter Crosby, both grew up in the small western Maine town of Strong. When they married they moved to nearby Phillips, where Thurza gave birth to Ezekiel in 1845, followed nine-and-a-half years later by Cornelia Thurza, born November 10, 1854. Lemuel tried various business ventures from a starch factory to a store, where, among other things, he brokered furs trapped in the region. But his health was always poor; before Cornelia turned two, he died of consumption—tuberculosis. Both she and Ezekiel, it seemed, inherited their father's sickly constitution. In that era, doctors advised that "delicate children" spend as much time as possible outdoors. Cornelia loved the woods and waterways around Phillips. For her, the fresh-air cure worked wonders, at least for a time. But Ezekiel didn't share her luck. In 1868, when he was only twenty-three, he, like his father, died of consumption. Cornelia, aged thirteen, and her mother were now the only Crosbys left. The bond between them remained very strong until Thurza's death in 1903.

Sometime in her teens, Cornelia inherited $600, most likely from her father. Showing levelheaded good sense—and the understanding that she'd probably need to be self-supporting—she invested the money in her own education. At the time, $600 paid for two years at an Episcopal girls' finishing and college preparatory school, St. Catherine's Hall, in Augusta, Maine. There, in the company of girls from well-connected families all over New England, Cornelia learned social graces and forged friendships that would help her throughout her life.

During much of the 1870s, Cornelia worked as a bank teller in Franklin County, not far from Phillips. She taught Sunday school at the Congregational Church and joined women's social organizations. But when her health failed, as it did periodically, she would spend months recuperating, unable to work. Sometime before 1878, she had an experience that would shape her future. She described it this way:

> . . . after long months of illness from a severe lung trouble, from which I was not expected to recover. . . . I was carried, one June day, to the very foot of Mount Blue. . . . Here at a farmhouse I was to try the healing power of nature. A brook full of trout came laughingly dancing down the mountainside, and from there I took my first trout, with an alder pole, it is true. . . .

By 1878, Cornelia was fishing at mile-long Tim Pond in the Rangeley Lakes region. Instead of a makeshift pole, she used a split-bamboo rod, the gift of its maker, Charles Wheeler of

Farmington. Although Rangeley Lake itself is only nine miles long, the Rangeley Lakes Region is an angler's dream: 112 lakes and ponds with names like Cupsuptic, Aziscoos, and Mooselookmeguntic.

In the early 1880s, Cornelia worked as a telegrapher in Phillips. More importantly, she spent as much time as she could during the season—May through October—fishing in the Rangeley Lakes and detailing her experiences in a column for the *Phillips Phonograph,* the town's first newspaper. During that period she had relapses of her lung condition, sometimes for long stretches. In spite of that, her journalism career was heating up. By the end of October, 1883, she was also Phillips' official reporter for *The Franklin Journal,* published in Farmington. Her editor at the *Phonograph,* O. M. Moore, was the first person to call her "Fly Rod." The name stuck, and "Fly Rod's Note Book" became a popular column. Her style was chatty and humorous, much like a personal letter. She had a knack for combining her own fishing adventures—and comic misadventures—with information about where to stay and social notes about the people who ran sporting camps as well as those who stayed there.

The 1880s was a time of economic upheaval for Maine. After a decade of stable, farm-based prosperity, young people had begun leaving family farms for manufacturing jobs in the cities, and parts of the state felt deserted. To offset revenue lost from hauling freight, the Maine Central Railroad began to encourage tourism, paying Fly Rod as the state's first recreational publicist to promote the "outdoor industry." Soon a slogan she'd developed—Maine, The Nation's Playground—was known all over the country.

In the Gilded Age of the 1890s, well-to-do visitors seeking the healthy life and natural beauty Fly Rod described flocked to western Maine, often fleeing cities that the Industrial Revolution had left clogged with polluted air and water. Families stayed at wilderness camps, usually in small rustic cabins with a central lodge where they took their meals. Called "sports" or "rusticators," these "soft adventurers" hired local fishing and hunting guides whom they followed into the wilds every morning. Women as well as men loved fly-fishing, a sport of finesse rather than brute strength, and in spite of the day's fashions (including tight corsets, floor-length skirts, and high-necked gauzy blouses), they managed to take to the woods. Through her larger-than-life example and her persuasive columns, Fly Rod pioneered women's active enjoyment of nature and championed the call for less restrictive clothing:

> Why should not a woman do her fair share of tramping, hunting, and fishing and ask no odds of the men? The time is past; I thank Providence, when it was thought unladylike for a woman to be a good shot or a skillful angler.

Here, in another of her columns, dated May 31, 1895, Fly Rod entertained herself and her readers by gently poking fun at a visiting "sport" while, no doubt, leaving both him and his wife eager for more:

> About the most delightful angler on the Monday train was Mrs. W. P. Whitehouse, wife of Judge Whitehouse of Augusta, who for the first time had been fishing at Rangeley. . . . The Judge one morning started off with his guide and said: "Don't suppose there is some old pole, a string, and a few worms and Mrs. W. could amuse herself fishing off the wharf while I go out and get a big trout?" Coming back at night with two little trout, the Judge found his wife had amused all the camp by landing [fifteen] two-pounders.

The seasonal rhythm of Fly Rod's life was well established by the mid 1890s. She worked at banks, if her health allowed it, from November through April and did some traveling around New England, though her home base was always Phillips. Once the ice thawed on Maine's lakes, she spent her summers at various fishing camps. She was among the first to promote catch-and-release fishing. In the summer of 1893, which she described as "the happiest and best of my life," she caught over 2,500 fish. Her one-day maximum was 200 fish—many of which she presumably released back into the water—and she held a record for most fish caught in the shortest amount of time: fifty-two trout in forty-four minutes. Fly Rod also traveled north and east in the fall for Maine's deer and moose hunting seasons, which she described in detail for her eager readers.

As Fly Rod's fame increased, so did her collection of fishing tackle, much of it donated by admirers and by companies who wanted her to mention their fishing equipment in her syndicated columns. In that sense, she was one of the first female professional athletes—like her friend Annie Oakley—with the equivalent of today's product endorsements. "I am a plain woman of uncertain age, standing six feet in my stockings," she once wrote. "I have earned my bread for a good many years doing the work of a bank clerk. I scribble a bit for various sporting journals, and I would rather fish any day than go to heaven."

During the winter of 1894, Fly Rod helped Harvard professor A. R. Sweetser organize the Greenville-Rangeley Camp, a natural history camp for boys, the first of its kind. That summer Fly Rod was in charge of excursions for the twenty-five campers from wealthy families. The next winter she busily organized Maine's contribution to the first Sportsmen's Exposition held at Madison Square Garden in May of 1895. The exhibit's centerpiece was a 10-by 13-foot log cabin, called "Camp Maine Central." A taxidermist from Bangor, Maine, supplied stuffed fish and animals, and there were hundreds of photographs to whet tourists' appetites.

Fly Rod, with her imposing height, mythic skills, and personal charisma, could have easily been perceived as threatening to the men with whom she fished and hunted, and to the increasingly powerful Maine Sportsmen's Fish and Game Association, of which she was the only female member. In fact, she met with the opposite reaction. Fly Rod made no secret of her anti-suffrage point of view; she didn't believe women should vote. While this seems at odds with the way she herself freely crossed traditional gender boundaries, it did allow her to work and travel easily with men and exert influence in areas about which she cared deeply, such as conservation measures to ensure the future of fish and game. It also meant she avoided the vitriol heaped upon active suffrage fighters such as Elizabeth Cady Stanton and Susan B. Anthony. In fact, Fly Rod's contributions to women's rights were important and lasting. In his master's thesis *Diana of the Maine Woods*, March O. McCubrey notes that Fly Rod presented Maine as:

> . . . Edenic for women as it offered them not just a retreat from the modern world but a retreat from restrictive social prohibitions. Women, when engaged in outdoor sports, could be liberated from their restrictive clothing. In some cases, especially after the turn of the century, women organized their own activities, free from the supervision of male relatives and friends. . . . Crosby thus helped to construct an atmosphere promoting female involvement in male oriented activities, a rare occurrence in the urban world.

In 1897, the Maine Fish and Game Association hired Fly Rod as a "special agent" to increase its membership rolls. She actively lobbied the Maine legislature on behalf of a state-run system for registering Maine guides and increasing the state's Fish and Game budget to $40,000. She also continued working for the Maine Central Railroad, organizing Maine's third exhibit at the Sportsmen's Exposition in New York.

One day that week, decked out in her green leather hunting outfit, Fly Rod hosted a "pink tea" for the Women's Press Club—only pink refreshments were served that afternoon, in the shadow of the world's largest mounted moose head. Later in the week, while handing out promotional flyers, Fly Rod received a telegram stating that the "Guide Bill" had passed the legislature. She was delighted. In the future, registered Maine guides would need to buy a license for one dollar a year and file a one-page annual report. In honor of her efforts to pass the bill and as a thank you for all she'd done for her state, she was given the very first license, though she never worked as an official Maine guide.

By now Fly Rod was busy full time—Maine's original booster. She organized the state's entry at the Boston Food Fair, a festival of cooking demonstrations and commercial food exhibits. Like a ringmaster in her famous green suit, Fly Rod presided over "Camp Aucocisco" and its cabin, stuffed deer, and 107-pound squash. The exhibit also included her mother, demonstrating spinning, and a beautiful Penobscot young woman, Lucy Nicolar, showing how to make baskets. Fly Rod was, as usual, the main attraction.

The Fourth Annual New York Sportsmen's Exposition, which started on January 12, 1898, was also an enormous success, with increasing numbers of women attending. In the fall of 1898, Fly Rod was hired to mount a display at the Eastern Maine Fair in Bangor—another triumph. But soon after that event closed, she was admitted to Portland Eye and Ear Hospital because of an injury suffered the previous spring. While boarding a train, her skirt had caught, and she was dragged several hundred feet. Her knee was badly wrenched in the accident. Apparently, tuberculosis then attacked the injury site, which resulted in surgery and months of inactivity.

Although she was sidelined for about two years, Fly Rod kept writing and managed to do some fishing while hobbling on a crutch. For the Sportsmen's Exposition of 1901, she represented the Washington County Railroad's "Sunrise Route," which brought tourists to eastern Maine's beautiful hills and lakes. Annie Oakley dropped by the Maine exhibit every day. The two friends now had even more in common than before. Not only were they both professional athletes—women who navigated successfully in what was considered "a man's world"—but they'd also both suffered debilitating injuries, gone through surgery, and endured long, painful months in the hospital.

The year 1903 was a very difficult one for Fly Rod. Her mother—her life's companion and strongest supporter—died in February after a long illness. Doctors ordered bed rest for Fly Rod because of frayed nerves and her bad knee. Though she lived with chronic pain, she kept writing for the *Maine Woods* and other national publications throughout the decade, advocating for wildlife preservation.

As the 1920s dawned, Fly Rod, now in her sixties, suffered increasingly poor health. When, by 1926, she lost sight in one eye and could no longer fish, hunt, or hike in the woods, her spirits plummeted. She spent the spring of 1926 in St. Mary's Hospital in Lewiston, Maine, "trying to regain from a nervous breakdown and heart trouble," as she described it. Fly Rod managed to rise from her own ashes, however. Because of the kindness of Catholic health workers and friends, she converted to Catholicism and returned to Phillips, to the Rangeley lakes, to write and enjoy nature as best she could.

In September of 1929, when she was seventy-five, Fly Rod described her daily life this way: "I am now crippled, nearly blind, and alone, living with pleasant memories of the days gone by, with gifts from friends and souvenirs from the past." But, according to one newspaper clipping, she still managed to fish the Rangeley lakes when she was over eighty.

Fly Rod still spent her summers in Phillips until close to the end. She died on Armistice Day, 1946, a day after her ninety-third birthday, and was buried in the Village Cemetery in Strong, next to her parents and brother.

Authors Julia A. Hunter and Earle G. Shettleworth Jr. end their biography, *Fly Rod Crosby: The Woman Who Marketed Maine*, with this evocation of Fly Rod's enduring appeal:

> She loved the life there [in Rangeley], and that love came through in her writing and her public appearances. She shared her own adventures with fishing rod and gun with her readers, and she also made a point of writing about the activities and successes of other women who came to the region for fishing and hunting, or to study or simply enjoy the local flora and fauna. Presenting herself as a woman who was an accomplished woodswoman, her message was clear: I have gone out and done this; it is wonderful; you can do it, too—come on, this is fun!

LILLIAN "LA NORDICA" NORTON
(1857–1914)

The Yankee Diva

$\mathcal{L}$illian Nordica, from the western Maine village of Farmington, was a renowned operatic soprano, "America's first international diva," when an interviewer happened to ask if she did needlepoint to calm her nerves before walking out on stage. No, she answered, she couldn't knit nor could she do multiplication tables, for that matter. "But patching is my specialty," she added. "I can put on a good New England patch as well as anybody."

For all her diamonds and sapphires, three turbulent marriages, and celebrated performances in the opera houses of New York, London, Paris, Milan, and St. Petersburg, Nordica never lost sight of her practical, plainspoken Maine roots. She only lived in Farmington until the age of seven, but it remained the solid footing upon which her life of stunning vocal achievement was built; it was the one place this citizen of the world referred to as "home."

Lillian Norton, called Lillie, was born on December 12, 1857, the sixth daughter of Amanda Allen and Edwin Norton, whose ancestors had ploughed the land outside Farmington. The fifth daughter was the original Lillian, but after she died at the age

Lillian Norton and her poodle, Turk

of two, her name passed to the next daughter, a custom of the time called "repeating." Edwin, Lillie's father, was not well suited to farming, and debt plagued the family, but still they managed to create a rich cultural climate for their daughters, full of music, literature, and languages. Lillie's mother was the family's mainstay, a dynamo of intelligence, tenacity, and ambition. "Give me a spoon," she once said, "and I won't hesitate to dig a tunnel through a mountain."

The youngest in a large family, Lillie was used to receiving little attention and early on learned to look out for her own interests. It was her older sister, Wilhelmina, nicknamed Willie, who seemed destined for a great singing career. In 1864, hoping to improve their fortunes, the family moved to Boston. At first they tried running a boarding house, then Edwin turned to photography, but nothing quite worked out as planned. Always resourceful, Amanda clerked at Jordan Marsh's department store. The family pinned its hopes on Willie's extraordinary soprano voice, which she developed at the newly founded New England Conservatory. At home, the entire family sang. Lillie was forever imitating Willie's scales and vocal exercises; in fact, she became such a pest that her family paid her a few pennies not to sing.

In the fall of 1868, the Nortons were visiting cousins in Farmington when heavy rains caused flooding of the nearby Sandy River. In the wake of the flood, sixteen-year-old Willie caught typhoid fever and died. The family plunged into mourning. While Willie's death dashed Amanda's high hopes of fame and fortune, it also opened the way for Lillie. For two years Amanda grieved, almost dead to the world, then suddenly, as if for the first time, she really listened to her youngest daughter sing.

Now the family's energies focused on Lillie. She was just fourteen when her long, difficult years of operatic training began, first at the New England Conservatory, where she studied with Willie's teacher, John O'Neill. Brilliant and inspiring, O'Neill was also such a taskmaster that Lillian was the only one of his original students to last the full four years, which she later described as "stained with tears and sodden with discouragement." But she, like her mother, never gave up hope and never stopped working hard. For all of the sacrifices Lillie made, however, she also felt transcendent joy. The aria "Visi d'Arte" ("I Live for Art") in Giacomo Puccini's opera, *Tosca*, might describe Lillie Norton's reality too: fully dedicating herself to the gift of an amazing voice.

While Lillie dreamed of one day singing in the world's great opera houses, her feet still stayed firmly planted on the ground. In the years she studied at the Conservatory, her family struggled; everyone worked just to survive. Lillie herself took a part-time job at a bookshop and spent her lunch hour walking the streets so that the other clerks wouldn't know she was too poor to afford a meal.

After graduation, Lillie, accompanied by her mother, left for New York, where she studied with Italian opera singer Madame Maretzek. By this time, two of the Norton daughters were married, and Edwin went to live with one of them. The Nortons were prepared to sacrifice even their house to further Lillian's career. To afford her continued lessons, Lillie soon was singing with Patrick Gilmore's band in Madison Square Garden. For $100 a week and expenses, including those of her mother, she joined Gilmore's tour of the West and, in 1877, traveled with him to Europe. For Lillie, singing in Dublin, London, and Paris felt like a grand opportunity, and the reviews were good.

In Paris, however, Lillie soon left the band, believing she needed to risk everything in pursuit of serious operatic training. Her schedule left little time to rest: she studied operatic acting with an elderly Frenchman, François Delsarte, and voice training with Emilio Belari, in addition to taking French lessons every day. Back in their tiny apartment, she practiced *Lucia di Lammermoor, La Traviata,*

Faust, and *Aida,* sometimes six hours a day, and taught several students of her own. When Delsarte died suddenly, Lillie and Amanda left for Italy, where Antonio Sangiovanni, a great teacher at the Conservatory of Milan, agreed to teach her for free.

Sangiovanni was kind, and Lillie made great progress with her singing. She was excited about her approaching debut as Donna Elvira in Mozart's opera *Don Giovanni;* still, the work was strenuous, the hours long, their apartment cold and dank. On March 10, 1879, Lillian stood in the wings, waiting for her cue, when the audience screamed the leading prima donna off the stage. Although Lillie's own singing won the audience's approval, most of the other leads were fired and the production scratched. Then it was on to Brescia, where she sang the role of Violetta in *La Traviata.* This time her singing caused a major sensation: Every aria was encored, adoring crowds rushed the footlights, bouquets of flowers showered the stage. The next morning a string band stood under the window of "La Nordica," serenading her with *Traviata's* overture. This was the success for which the whole Norton family had worked and sacrificed.

But success still exacted a price. Lillian and her mother weren't able to spend the summer in Farmington and Boston as they'd hoped. Edwin, who had not fully recovered after an explosion at his photographic studio, nevertheless urged his wife and daughter to stay in Europe. In spite of homesickness and financial troubles, the family remained intact; they exchanged long letters and, now, newspaper articles about La Nordica.

That fall Lillie was hired to sing ten secondary roles at the Imperial Opera in St. Petersburg, Russia. Although she'd already memorized sixteen roles, none of these was in the Opera's repertoire. With only six weeks before the season started, Lillie learned all the new parts. Her performances met with such wild acclaim that Amanda, in constant letters home, could hardly contain herself:

In *The Huguenots* . . . she comes on the scene mounted on a great elegant white horse, led by two grooms, and accompanied by two attendants on black horses. The music and scene of this opera surpass description!!! Every possible combination of scenic effect is brought to bear on this, the whole theatre is lighted with *electric lights* and the instrumentation of the *imperial orchestra* is grand beyond imagination and poor little *Lilly Norton* rides onto the scene with as much dignity and coolness as ever did the original—and the papers said she sang as no Queen could sing.

As ambitious as Amanda was for her daughter, the years away from New England weighed heavily on her heart. Edwin's health suffered, she had not yet met her grandchildren, and she was afraid she'd die without ever seeing Farmington again. But Lillie's desire to give her father a financially comfortable old age had borne fruit, and this was a comfort. The Imperial Opera was so pleased with La Nordica that they offered her $2,500 to sing for the following winter season. Always an astute businesswoman, Lillie held out for $4,000—and received it.

Later that first winter, terrible news arrived from Boston. Edwin had died on Christmas Eve. Both mother and daughter had hoped so keenly to return home that summer and share their success with Edwin, but now it was too late. They pressed on. Lillie sang in Europe and back in St. Petersburg for a second winter. Never content to rest, she signed on with the Paris Opera, realizing another of her ambitions. But this meant learning French and the French opera repertoire. Not only did Lillie become the prima donna of the Paris season, couturiers named a new color, as well as a new cloak, "La Nordica." At last Lillie and her mother were living a life of luxury. Opera stars of that era were treated like royalty; it was not unusual for admirers to give them diamonds and other expensive jewelry.

While in Paris that season of 1882, Lillian received a check for $10,000 and later a proposal of marriage from Frederick Allen Gower, a second cousin whom she'd met once many years before. Cousin Fred had grown into a handsome and important international businessman and reputed partner of Alexander Graham Bell. At Frederick's insistence, Lillie broke her contract with the Paris Opera for a forfeit of $10,000 so that they could be married in May of 1883. Frederick Gower was so wealthy the money seemed a trivial matter. In September, Lillie, her new husband, and her mother sailed for home. After a wonderful family reunion and concert in Farmington, however, Lillie found herself without singing engagements.

Her New York City debut, on November 26, 1883, in *Faust*—billed as Lillian Norton Gower—received only lukewarm reviews. For her next performance, she returned to the name Nordica. Some of the Boston papers criticized her voice, but Lillie dazzled Chicago. The triumph was short-lived, however, when Frederick Gower—who'd been traveling on business—suddenly reappeared and whisked Lillie back to New York, supposedly angry that she'd received only second billing. Because of Frederick's insistence that Lillie break her contract with the Paris Opera, her career in France seemed over, and now her American tour had ended too.

Amanda had grown to despise her son-in-law, as it became more clear that he hated opera and didn't want his wife to sing at all—even at home. His violent outbursts terrified Lillie, and when he ordered Amanda out of his London house, Lillie went with her. Lillian's mental and physical health broke down. Back in Boston, she petitioned the courts for independent income on grounds of abuse, allegations Frederick planned to fight. But, in July of 1885, he disappeared on an experimental balloon flight across the English

Channel and was never seen again. It turned out that he'd managed to squander his fortune as well.

Six months after she was widowed, Lillie returned to performing on a well-received American tour, and then she and her mother set sail for England. There, Lillie learned the English oratorio style and became the toast of London, singing with the world-famous tenor, Jean de Reszke. While she enjoyed the life of a prima donna in London, she was never content unless pursuing a new dream: She'd long wanted to perform at the Bayreuth Festival in Germany, where Richard Wagner's operas were presented—and where no American had ever been invited to sing.

In 1891, while keeping up a rigorous schedule of operas and concerts in London, Lillie happened to sing with the young Hungarian baritone, Zoltan Dome, who'd made a splash that season. They were attracted to each other, but she felt wary of marriage, and each had a career to nurture.

Amanda Norton, who'd soldiered on at her daughter's side year after year, far from home, finally died on November 28, 1891, a bitter loss for Lillie. Her London apartment felt empty without the constant companionship of her mother, best friend, wisest critic, and staunchest admirer. Having grown up in a big family, Lillie longed for a lively household, wished she had children, and missed her parents, sisters, nieces, and nephews, to whom she'd always felt close. But she had her singing, and it was her life.

In November of 1893, Lillie appeared as a regular member of the Metropolitan Opera in New York. Then Richard Wagner's widow, Cosima, a zealous protector of his work, invited her to appear at Bayreuth, Germany, in the summer of 1894, singing the role of Elsa in *Lohengrin.* Lillie knew the opera, but in Italian not German, and mastering Cosima's staging methods as well as the German language meant months of study. Still, Lillie was happy to achieve another of her dreams, and not just for her own sake:

Zoltan Dome was hired to sing the role of Parsifal. Lillie's Elsa moved and delighted German audiences, including Cosima Wagner. Blinded—and apparently deafened—by love, however, Lillie imagined Dome's Parsifal was also wonderful, but few others shared that judgment, and his career at Bayreuth quickly ended. Nevertheless, Nordica and Dome were soon engaged, although Lillie seemed in no rush to marry—as if she were waiting for Zoltan to prove himself. In the meantime, she pursued her own career with zeal.

For all her level-headedness and discipline when it came to singing, Lillie was foolhardy in her romantic life. Suddenly, in the spring of 1896, Dome arrived in Indianapolis, where Lillie had been appearing, and insisted that they be married. During the seven years their marriage lasted, Zoltan Dome was vain and lazy, and a notorious philanderer. Finally, after one too many proofs of his infidelity, Lillian sued for divorce.

As the years passed and Lillian neared fifty, she knew that her singing days were numbered. Instead of reducing her concerts, however, she increased them with a triumphant tour of the United States. Not simply a legendary singer and renowned personality, she was now an institution. Her image—considered the height of American elegance and beauty—appeared in Coca-Cola advertising campaigns of the period. During the fall and winter of 1907, Lillie gave nearly sixty concerts in fifty cities and small towns. For all of them, she wore evening gowns designed by the House of Worth, draped herself in jewels, and sang beloved arias and songs.

In July of 1908, Nordica married for the third time, this time to a millionaire named George Washington Young, who'd sent her an emerald necklace after attending one of her concerts. The Youngs honeymooned in France, then sailed to New York, and Lillie again toured the country. During this trip she talked to many women dedicated to the suffrage movement, and she herself became an ardent suffragist. She also decided to wear only American-made gowns. Whenever she could, she spoke out in favor of women gaining the vote and earning equal pay for equal work.

In August of 1911, Lillie and George visited Farmington. For her birthday, her sisters had bought and repaired the little family farmhouse, a gift she greatly loved. She was happy to give a concert for free in her beloved hometown. On August 17, horses, buggies, and motorcars lined the streets of Farmington, and the auditorium filled long before the concert began. Ferns and goldenrod, picked from nearby fields, decorated the stage. The next day newspapers around the country trumpeted the event: "Familiar Old Songs Move Her Fellow Townspeople to Tears. . . . Weatherbeaten farmers and their wives sat in the audience and accorded the singer one of the most heartfelt tributes she has ever received. . . ."

George Young was an aggressive businessman, but early in their marriage, his affairs began to unravel and he lost vast amounts of money. Time and again, Lillie came to the rescue. Meanwhile, she was as busy as ever, but any illusions she had about George soon vanished. When she admitted, "I'm a poor picker of husbands," no one disagreed. Also at this time, the knowledge that her vocal powers would soon wane sometimes rose like a shadow, though her voice remained quite strong and expressive. To escape her unhappy home, as well as to challenge herself while she could still sing, Lillie organized a concert tour of Australia and New Zealand in the summer of 1913.

The schedule was demanding, and Lillie fell ill in Australia, but she managed to put on grand performances and decided to continue on to Java as she'd originally planned. The train from Sydney to Melbourne on December 17 was so late that she almost missed the *Tasman*'s sailing. But when her manager sent a telegram to the captain, he held the ship in port. Unfortunately, ten days later, the *Tasman* hit a coral reef and stuck there until another ship pulled it free. Lillie kept her courage, but before the ship could limp to the nearest port, hurricane winds and rains blasted it, and Lillie developed pneumonia. For three months she languished on remote Thursday Island, plagued by fevers. She recovered enough to sail for Batavia, but then, early on the morning of May 10, 1914, she whispered, "I am coming, Mother," and died. She was fifty-seven.

Although Lillie had just drafted a new will, few of her last wishes were honored, except her desire to be cremated. The money she wanted to share with her sisters was eaten up by legal expenses. La Nordica was one of the last great nineteenth-century opera divas, a star from the Golden Age, and people everywhere mourned her passing, but it seemed that she might be forgotten as World War I engulfed Europe and the United States.

But Farmington, Maine, would never forget Lillie Norton. In 1927, townspeople bought the farmhouse where she was born, renovated the property, and opened the Nordica Homestead Museum. Open every summer, the museum "displays many artifacts from her extraordinary career, including original gorgeous stage gowns and dazzling tiaras and jewelry, as well as her entire collection of opera scores." On March 17, 1943, the Yankee Diva received another honor: the USS *Lillian Nordica* was launched at South Portland, Maine, the first Liberty Ship named for a musical artist.

JOSEPHINE DIEBITSCH PEARY

(1863–1955)

Arctic Explorer & Writer

On the afternoon of September 6, 1909, the ink-blue waters of the Atlantic lapped at the rocky shores of Eagle Island in Casco Bay, Maine. As clouds drifted down the sky, they built, wave upon wave, into horses and trains and fields of candy snow. A "typical Maine day"—so beautiful, hard-won and precious.

The sun was strong enough to warm Josephine Peary's back as she bent to cut pink and white phlox for a bouquet, but the light had already tipped toward blue, signaling a change. In the garden crickets sang, *hurry, hurry; time is short.* There would be more fine, summerlike days before she, her sixteen-year-old daughter, Marie Ahnighito, and six-year-old son, Robert Jr., left the island for the winter, but a cool, bright wind, fresh from Canada, kept the temperatures in the sixties, a reminder of what was to come.

So many times that day, Josephine's thoughts flew north as they always did, beyond the wind, beyond Canada, to northernmost Greenland and the Arctic Circle. For twenty-three years, her husband, Robert E. Peary, had searched for the North Pole. She had accompanied him on three expeditions and met him several times in Greenland. A respected Arctic explorer in her own right,

Josephine Diebitsch Peary

she was also a renowned writer and lecturer. But now she waited. It had been months since she'd heard from her husband. After so many failed attempts, had he reached the North Pole? Was he still alive? She knew the dangers. She'd lived them herself: blinding snowstorms, the disorientation of endless white and gray, crevasses that swallowed dogs and sledges, cold beyond any cold imaginable, nights that lasted half a year. You must get used to waiting, people assumed. You never get used to waiting, Josephine knew.

Holding the spicy-smelling phlox, Josephine rose to her feet. She couldn't let herself imagine disaster. Instead, she admired the bay gleaming like wet gold. Among the lobster boats and day sailers, she saw two motorboats heading toward the island from the direction of South Harpswell, on the far shore. She wasn't expecting visitors. Robert had bought Eagle Island in 1881, and theirs was its only house, built high on granite bluffs, like the pilothouse of a ship sailing northeasterly. For a moment, Josephine's heart beat faster. Maybe there was some word. But no, it couldn't be.

In a few moments, the first boat tied up at the island's mooring. A man scrambled into a skiff and rowed to shore, eager to deliver a telegram into Josephine's hand. She dropped the flowers and nervously ripped open the envelope. Inside was a message from the Associated Press: *Peary has reached the Pole.* The man could hardly contain himself, but Josephine didn't get overly excited. Too many false alarms had made her wary. Soon the second boat dropped anchor, and another man, red faced and sweating, ran up the lawn. It was Mr. Palmer, the storekeeper and postmaster of South Harpswell. He also carried a telegram, this one from Peary himself: "Have made it at last. . . ."

On April 6, 1909, he had planted the U.S. flag at 90 degrees north latitude: the first man, he believed, to stand at the top of the world. It had taken him five more months to reach Indian Harbor, Labrador, from where he cabled his accomplishment.

Soon other newspapermen swarmed Eagle Island. Josephine could hardly believe it. All those years; now success. And Robert would be coming home soon, for good, she hoped. At last!

"What do you say now, Mrs. Peary?" one reporter asked.

A woman of great dignity but also high spirits, Josephine responded, "I say, come on, boys, let's have a drink."

Josephine, born in Washington, D.C., on May 22, 1863, was the eldest daughter of wealthy and well-educated parents, Herman Henry Diebitsch of Prussia and Magdelena Augusta Schmid Diebitsch of Saxony. Herman taught languages at the Smithsonian Institution, a vibrant center for learning of all kinds. Jo, as she preferred to be called, had two younger brothers, Emil and Henry, and a younger sister, Marie, nicknamed Mayde. Hers was a loving, cultured family, one that encouraged her curiosity and independence. As a girl she was an avid reader. "I always revered learning and scientific investigation and intellectual victories," she would later write. After graduating from public high school in Washington, she studied at a business college, then worked as a clerk in the exchange department of the Smithsonian. Pictures from the era show an elegantly dressed young woman with full lips, thick dark hair, and firm eyebrows highlighting a frank, steady gaze. A "belle of the capital" as W. H. Hobbs, a Robert Peary biographer, described her, Josephine was not only beautiful and adventurous, she also had a firm, practical bent and a strong will, qualities that would be tested again and again in future years.

In 1885, while attending dancing school, Jo met Robert Edwin Peary, a handsome, twenty-nine-year-old Navy civil engineer, who'd grown up in Portland, Maine, and graduated from Bowdoin College. For three years, they courted, much of it by mail, while "Bert" organized a survey for a possible canal in Nicaragua, and, in 1887, traveled to Greenland for the first time. On August 11, 1888, when Jo was twenty-five, the two were married at the

Diebitsch's stately Washington home. According to tradition, the groom selected the bride's bouquet, usually made of white flowers. But that afternoon, as the temperature hit 101 degrees, Jo carried—at her own insistence—a handful of red roses instead.

Jo and Bert lived in New York, then Philadelphia, where he worked on various Naval civil engineering projects. But his northern adventure had sparked other dreams, which Josephine shared: to cross Greenland's ice cap and find the North Pole. The Pearys were not alone in their ambitions. By the 1870s, the United States had at least partially recovered from the devastation of the Civil War, and its focus shifted outward to explore—and dominate—unknown worlds. Now Americans joined Italians and Norwegians in search of the same prize: to claim for their own countries the exact spot, on a flowing sea of ice, where every direction is south: the geographic North Pole. The race was on.

Soon after their wedding, Robert Peary began actively organizing an expedition to reach the northern end of Greenland via the inland route. He found sponsorship from the American Geographical Society, the Brooklyn Institute, and the Philadelphia Academy of Sciences. Not only was Josephine central in planning for the trip, she also helped raise money. She wasn't shy about tapping her family's many connections at the Smithsonian and in Washington, D.C., nor did she have any intention of waving to Robert's ship as it disappeared below the horizon.

In June of 1891, a party of seven explorers set sail from New York bound for Greenland on the steam-powered whaling barkentine, *Kite.* Jo was among them, the first woman ever to take part in an Arctic expedition. Other members included Eivind Astrup, a Norwegian skier; Frederick A. Cook, a surgeon; and Matthew Henson, Peary's African-American valet. Newspapers, eagerly following the story, reported that Peary was "crazy" for bringing along a woman and a black man. Such attitudes helped forge a strong friendship between Jo and Henson, who would become perhaps the most highly skilled explorer on Peary's team.

Jo's resolve was tried early on when Peary broke his leg on shipboard. She nursed him and cooked for the whole group, as well as tended Redcliffe House, the two-room home they built on the shores of McCormick Bay, halfway between the Arctic Circle and the North Pole. Within a few weeks—before ice locked it in place for the winter—the *Kite* sailed south, not to return for a year. The small party was alone now, dependent on each other for companionship and survival. One day, while Robert was still recovering from his leg fracture, the group went by boat to hunt walruses. In their excitement they ran aground on an ice floe, where some 250 aggressive walruses attacked the boat. Jo crouched down to protect Robert's vulnerable leg with her own body; meanwhile, she calmly loaded the men's rifles as they fired shot after shot. Jo's calmness and hands-on courage that day won the men's admiration. She earned their devotion by preparing special feasts to celebrate each birthday and holiday, when, so far from home, spirits sagged.

During that year Jo grew to be a skilled hunter of reindeer, ptarmigan, and other game, which the party needed for clothing as well as for food. She tended her own trap lines, kept a sidearm, and was a fine shot with her Winchester rifle. She was interested in everything—wildflowers, glaciers, Inuit customs—and she kept scrupulous notes about the expedition, published in 1901 as the groundbreaking work, *My Arctic Journal: A Year Among Ice-Fields and Eskimos.*

At first Jo shared the common American prejudices of her era; she described the Inuits as "smelly," "odd" people, uncultured and uncouth. But soon her curiosity, friendliness, and sense of humor—and theirs—carried the day. She realized quickly that the expedition's only chance at success lay in adapting the Inuits' survival techniques. She learned their language and asked the women to teach her how to make Arctic clothing. Though she wouldn't chew the skins to soften them, as the Inuits did, she used their patterns, spending hours working with them to make bearskin pants, snowshoe hare stockings, waterproof sealskin boots, fur coats, and mittens of deerskin.

In 1893, pregnant with her first child, Jo again set sail with Robert on a larger expedition: the goal, to explore land north of Greenland, and again, if possible, reach the North Pole. Their base of operations that year was Anniversary House, a small building on Greenland's Bowdoin Bay. It was here, in September, that she delivered her daughter, Marie Ahnighito Peary, the first white child born that far north, at less than 13 degrees from the North Pole. The name "Ahnighito" honored the Inuit woman who made the baby's first fur suit. Marie was nicknamed "The Snow Baby" for her startling snow-colored skin and northerly birthplace.

During that winter, living in darkness except for the light of oil lamps, Jo fed her daughter and rocked her to sleep inside Anniversary House. Then in February, the sun finally rose over the mountains, flooding Bowdoin Bay with light. Jo placed Ahnighito in the middle of a bed heaped with furs. Here sunlight, shining through a high window, touched the baby's skin. Eagerly, she stretched out her fingers to meet the strange bright beams, "just as if she was bathing in perfumed golden water," Josephine wrote. "It was the first time she had ever seen the sun."

While Robert stayed on for another two years, Jo sailed home the following summer. Her parents, brothers, and sister had yet to meet Marie Ahnighito, who was already toddling and saying words. Robert returned home in 1896. A year later, Josephine and Marie Ahnighito returned with him to Bowdoin Bay. Jo recorded the events of Marie's first year and her visit to her birthplace in a very popular children's book, *The Snow Baby*, published in 1901. As she had done in *My Arctic Journal*, she was able to recreate the wonders and hardships of the northern world she was beginning to know well. *The Snow Baby* is full of information about Arctic landscape and animal life, as well as Inuit culture. It shows Jo's interest in science and human nature, and her lyrical eye for detail. In this passage, she describes summer's coming:

> The great sheet of snow-covered sea-ice over which the hunters had driven their dogs and sledges was beginning to soften under the caresses of the summer sun. Pools of water began to collect like cool green shadows on the white rolling surface, while numerous black specks on the white sheet showed where sleeping seals were sunning themselves beside their front doors, which opened in the deep sea.

Separated by thousands of miles during much of their married life, Jo and Bert tried to keep in touch by letter. Often she would make five copies of a single letter and send them off on five different whaling ships, in hopes that one might reach her husband. For months, sometimes years, she had no idea if he were even alive.

In a letter dated March 1900, and written from their home on Twelfth Street NW, Washington, D.C., Jo told Robert about the death of their second child, a tragedy she'd had to face alone. Here, in words meant only for him, we can glimpse the private toll their life exacted. "If only the time since last August has not been as hard for you as it has for me is all I ask & pray for mightily," she told him.

> Surely we ought not both to suffer & I have suffered for both. Our little darling, whom you never knew was taken from me on Aug 7, '99 just 7 months after she came. She was only sick a few days but the disease took

right hold of her little head & nothing could be done for her. . . . But oh my husband I wanted you, how much you will never know. I shall never feel quite the same again, part of me is in the little grave. The news of your terrible suffering came soon after. . . . It nearly prostrated me, but you know I am strong & can bear & bear & bear.

Soon after writing this letter, Jo organized her own expedition to help Peary recuperate from his "terrible suffering," the amputation of eight frostbitten toes. She and Marie Ahnighito were forced to overwinter 300 miles south of Peary's camp, however, when their ship, the *Windward*, struck an iceberg en route. That same winter, Jo met Peary's pregnant Inuit lover, Allakasingwah. In spite of the pain this must have caused her, she remained supportive of his work in every possible way.

Once the Pearys' son, Robert Jr., was born in 1903, Josephine no longer traveled north. Robert grew increasingly obsessed and single-minded, and the weight of his failure to reach the Pole wore him down. Jo published articles about her own Arctic adventures, as well as his, and gave illustrated lectures to raise money, keeping his quest in the public eye. On September 6, 1909, when the telegram announcing his success arrived on Eagle Island, it was a shared victory, a family triumph.

Although Peary was the Charles Lindbergh of his day, incredibly famous and admired, he was also dogged by controversy. Another explorer, Dr. Frederick A. Cook, the surgeon who'd set Peary's leg in 1891, insisted that he'd reached the North Pole first, in April of 1908. The controversy swept scientific circles and reached the general public, who first sided with Cook, until a group commissioned by the National Geographic Society agreed that Peary's claim was the more believable. (In the 1980s, new calculations indicated that probably neither Peary nor Cook had reached the geographic North Pole, but the issue remains unresolved.)

At last, once the Navy had granted Peary the status of rear admiral, and an admiral's retirement, he put Arctic exploration behind him. The family now spent summers on Eagle Island together. Robert became interested in aviation and the uses that planes might have in defending the country. After his death from pernicious anemia in 1920, Jo moved from Washington to Portland, Maine, for the winters. Summers she lived on Eagle Island with her children and grandchildren.

Reflecting on her life, Jo once told a reporter, "I have looked on the Frozen Deep as an old friend, as well as a vast phenomenon to be solved." The Peary family's connection with the Arctic was a profound and lasting one. Their daughter, Marie Ahnighito Peary Stafford, wrote books about the Arctic—several with her mother as co-author—and promoted her father's accomplishments. Robert E. Peary Jr. was a civil engineer and an Arctic explorer as well. In 1955, the National Geographic Society awarded Josephine its highest honor, the Medal of Achievement. That same year, on December 19, she died at home—290 Baxter Boulevard, in Portland—at the age of ninety-two. She was buried next to her husband in Arlington National Cemetery.

Not long after her death, Jo's children donated Eagle Island to the state of Maine. During the summer, it's still open to the public, a beautiful rocky place with trails and wide vistas of ocean and sky. The house serves as a museum, full of family memorabilia and Arctic treasures from fur skins to narwhal tusks, from photographs to Inuit tools and clothing. Jo's presence still graces Eagle Island. Her own words, published over a hundred years ago in *My Arctic Journal*, evoke the extraordinary woman she was:

. . . two very old women in particular were led to me, and one of them, putting her face close to mine . . . scrutinized me carefully from head to foot, and then said slowly, "Uwanga sukinuts ammissuare, koona immartu ibly takoo nahme," which means, "I have lived a great many suns, but never have seen anything like you."

FLORENCE NICOLAR SHAY

(1884–1960)

Penobscot Basketmaker & Tribal Advocate

*F*lorence sat in the workroom adjoining her kitchen, weaving a basket of brown ash splints and sweet grass. Nestled on her lap was the basket's base, which she'd shaped around a wooden mold, smoothed down by generations of use. She wove quickly and steadily. Hers were practiced hands. She was seventy-four, and she'd been making baskets since girlhood, a skill and an art—as well as a tool for economic survival—passed down from her mother and her mother's mother.

It was mid-January, 1958. While she worked, Florence listened to her favorite Saturday radio broadcast of classical music. A Chopin sonata was playing. Only 3:00 P.M. and already sunlight had turned to slanting gold. In just a week she and Leo would celebrate their fiftieth wedding anniversary. For a moment her fingers grew still as she gazed out the window at the Penobscot River, which surrounded Indian Island, part of the Penobscot reservation where she'd spent most of her life. Always the river beckoned—pathway, source of food and livelihood, spiritual heartbeat. It had

Florence Nicolar Shay

been frozen since November, and on its white expanse, wind had sculpted snow into peaked waves and long blue shadows, stark and elegant as eagle wings. Upriver, beyond the mills of Old Town, the sun's oblique rays glittered through the geometry of bare tree branches. She picked up an ash splint, which she'd dyed herself, the deep blue of predawn. Chopin's music danced. Gold sunlight touched her white hair, the blue splint.

Florence's calm industry belied another part of her makeup, not so apparent to someone watching her weave a basket that afternoon: her boldness on behalf of the Penobscot people. "This feisty lady had had the temerity to write to President Franklin Delano Roosevelt and complain that the State of Maine had taken away her right to vote," says historian Neil Rolde in his book, *Unsettled Past, Unsettled Future: The Story of Maine Indians.* Florence, herself, in a fifteen-page booklet called *History of the Penobscot Tribe,* written and self-published in 1933, described the situation with characteristic clarity and honest fire:

> In 1924, during President Coolidge's administration, an act was passed by Congress conferring citizenship upon all Indians born within the territorial limits of the United States. My husband and I and our family lived in Connecticut from 1923 to 1930. During the presidential election of 1928, we registered as citizens of the United States and voted as such with no questions asked as to our right. After we returned to Maine, we, with my sister, went to the registration board of Old Town, Maine, to register as citizens in our home town, but we were met with a distinct refusal, as an obsolete law of the State of Maine forbids the registration and voting by Indians, and in that law we are classed with criminals, paupers, and morons.

After the United States entered World War II—and Maine Indians were still denied suffrage—Florence added this protest to the 1942 reissue of her booklet: "I have four sons and I feel the government has not the right to draft my boys without giving us the right to vote. . . . We are a segregated, alienated people and many of us are beginning to feel the weight of the heel that is crushing us to nothingness. . . ."

But Florence didn't simply write pamphlets and letters, then passively wait for a response. In spite of her personal reticence, she was an activist, following a long family tradition, lived out in her own unique way.

Florence Estelle Nicolar entered the world on August 5, 1884, at Indian Island, the youngest of three daughters born to Joseph and Elizabeth Josephs Nicolar. One sister, Emma, was already fourteen when Florence was born; Lucy was two. The girls' parents were a remarkable couple. Joseph came from an impressive line of Penobscots, among them John Neptune, a powerful chief elected lieutenant governor for life in 1816. Joseph himself was a very intelligent, educated man, who served more terms as tribal representative to the state legislature than any other Penobscot. In addition to land surveying, farming, hunting, and fishing, he wrote feature stories about Penobscot culture and history. In 1893, he wrote and published a book entitled *The Life and Traditions of the Red Man.*

Florence's mother, Elizabeth Nicolar, called Lizzie, was also a powerhouse. Twenty-one years younger than Joseph, she was smart, beautiful, and skilled not only at making baskets but at promoting their sales, a gifted leader and organizer. Florence and her sisters were raised in an intellectually ambitious and political family. This strong foundation bolstered them for the years they would spend advocating for educational, economic, and social justice for their tribe.

For thousands of years, the Penobscots had roamed freely over a vast territory in the Penobscot River watershed. No boundaries, no state lines, no reservations. With three other woodlands tribes in the Northeast—the Passamaquoddy, Mik'maq, and Maliseet—they formed the Wabanaki Confederation. The Wabanakis followed nature's rhythms. In the winter they lived in small settlements scattered throughout the region's forests. In late spring they canoed to the coast, escaping insects and enjoying summer's bounty of fish, shellfish, and berries. In 1797, the Penobscot tribe deeded most of what is now Maine to Massachusetts—before the two became separate states. In return, their reservation consisted of 140 small islands in the Penobscot River between Old Town and Mattawamkeag, and they were to receive annual monetary and other subsidies. But these soon stopped: Treaty conditions were broken, promises betrayed.

During Florence's lifetime, the seasonal rhythm of her forebears remained, motivated now by economic necessity. The fall, winter, and spring months were spent on Indian Island, where she and her sisters attended the Catholic mission primary school. Lizzie taught them how to make baskets, and they organized sweetgrass braiding parties with other island women. The Nicolars' was a lively household, filled with music and laughter. Many Penobscots played musical instruments, so impromptu concerts were common, as well as lectures and other events held at the church. Florence loved playing the piano and practiced the hours it took to become an excellent musician.

In the summer, along with many other Penobscots from Indian Island, the Nicolars joined the seasonal migration to the Maine coast. With them on the train, they brought the baskets they'd made during the winter, as well as fresh supplies. Different families selected different resort communities. Florence's returned each year to Kennebunkport in southern Maine. There they set up a stand, selling baskets and making new ones. To attract more tourists, Lizzie encouraged Florence and Lucy to sing and dance.

Dressed in traditional Indian outfits, they entertained potential customers. Lucy especially enjoyed this. Around the first of August, when their baskets sold out, the Nicolars returned to Indian Island.

In 1894, when Florence was only ten, her father died—a deep loss for the family and the tribe. Because Lizzie and the girls now had to support themselves, astute marketing of their baskets was essential. Soon, the three began taking part in sportsmen's exhibitions in Boston, New York, and Baltimore. These extravaganzas featured displays of sporting gear and wilderness equipment. Maine's exhibit promoted not only sporting goods but a way of life: "rusticating," the kind of wilderness tourism for which the state was becoming famous. The encampment included a log cabin with stuffed moose and deer, Maine guides, and a small artificial lake. Noted sportswoman Cornelia "Fly Rod" Crosby was there, demonstrating fly-fishing, while nearby, the Nicolars made baskets and snowshoes. While Lizzie and her daughters played into white Americans' notions concerning the romantic exoticism of Indians (whom they lumped together into a single image of Plains-type western tribes), much to their credit, they did it with a clear-eyed sense of economic purpose and a desire to preserve their own distinct culture and traditions.

Florence was thirteen or fourteen when Lucy left for Boston to go to high school and study voice. Lucy then toured as "Princess Watahwaso" ("Bright Star"), singing, acting, and lecturing about Indian cultures, while Florence remained at home. Although the leap from Indian Island's mission primary school to public high school on the mainland often proved rocky for the few Penobscots who tried it, Florence adapted well and in 1906, at the age of twenty-two, she graduated from Old Town High. Still eager for education, she attended Shaw Business College in Bangor, 12 miles away. She was a quick study at the skills needed for secretarial work, one of few professions open to any woman at the time, let alone a Penobscot.

On January 25, 1908, Florence married Leo Shay. He was a bright and industrious fellow, also from Indian Island, and six years her junior. While living on the island, they had seven children: Winter, born in approximately 1909 (who died of appendicitis at sixteen); Hattie, born in 1910 or 1911; Lawrence William, called Billy, in 1912; Martha Doris, known as Madeline or Maddy, in 1916; Lucille, a few years later; and Thomas Leo in 1921. Another daughter died in infancy.

In spite of the couple's hard work, it was almost impossible to make a living on Indian Island or in nearby Old Town. Jobs were scarce; prejudice against hiring native people further shrank their prospects. Therefore, in 1923, the year her mother died, Florence moved with Leo to Connecticut. Florence was adamant that her children grow up with economic and educational chances unavailable on the reservation. Part of being a Penobscot mother in that era, she believed, meant training her offspring to compete in the white world, as her own mother had taught her to survive by making baskets. The Shay children were raised speaking English, the language of opportunity, another way in which Florence prepared them to be self-sufficient.

In Connecticut, Florence had two more sons: Charles Norman in June of 1924 and Patrick Joseph in May of 1926. While raising a family, she did office work at Chief Two Moons Laboratory in Waterbury. Chief Two Moons, a Lakota Sioux shaman, ran a successful business selling herbal remedies in drugstores and by mail order. When the Great Depression hit, however, jobs dried up, so Florence and her family returned to Indian Island. They moved into the two-story house where she'd grown up. Her sister Lucy also came back home with her future third husband, "Chief" Bruce Poolaw, a Kiowa and fellow entertainer, twenty-one years younger than she, with whom she'd been traveling on the vaudeville circuit. Lucy had a house built on the riverbank, facing Old Town. A decade or so later, she and Bruce created a two-story teepee gift shop next-door.

Times were tough on the island. Grinding poverty caused many hardships, and there were few chances for either a living wage or a sound education—troubles compounded by the island's isolation and the Penobscots' status as second-class citizens. Joining her sisters, Lucy and Emma, and her sister-in-law, Pauline Shay, Florence set out to help. They resuscitated the Indian Woman's Club, of which their mother had been a founder thirty-five years earlier. Its purpose: to promote "Indian welfare, education and social progress." Soon they were again affiliated with the Maine Federation of Women's Clubs, as well as with the National Federation.

The first issue the women tackled was the right to educational opportunity. Not satisfied with the quality of the Indian Island school for her own family, Florence wanted all Penobscot children to have the option to attend Old Town's public schools. In 1931, the Maine legislature passed such a bill into law. But it came at a price. The women were "expelled" from the island's Catholic church for challenging the status quo. Finally, after a difficult struggle, a group of Penobscots, including Florence, was able to establish a Baptist church on the island.

Each summer, starting in the early 1930s, Florence brought her baskets to the Maine coast, as she'd done in childhood. She and Leo set up a tent store, The Indian Camp Basket Shop, on Route One in Lincolnville Beach, between Belfast and Camden on Penobscot Bay. Helped by Leo and the children, she spent her days weaving baskets and selling them to tourists, a mainstay of the family's income. Florence's son, Billy Shay, eventually carried on the family tradition. Caron Shay, Billy's daughter, a master basketmaker like her father and grandmother, observes that Florence's baskets were beautiful to look at and beautifully made, "known for their symmetry, fine craftsmanship, and lasting quality." She also created her own dyes, now a vanishing art.

As busy as Florence was raising a large family and weaving baskets, she made time to advocate for two other long-time dreams, besides better education: Indian suffrage and a bridge connecting Indian Island to the mainland. For generations, Penobscots had traveled back and forth to Old Town in a fourteen-passenger rowboat. The fare was two cents each way. With its brick and frame buildings, its church spires and smokestacks, Old Town was home to paper and textile mills. Each winter Penobscots would spread a thick trail of sawdust on the ice so they could travel back and forth to work, attend school, and buy supplies. Sometimes the trip was perilous: in spring, before ice-out when thin spots broke through; in late fall, when a sudden thaw eroded yesterday's solid track. There were accidents, drownings. During other seasons, when storms raged, the little ferry wouldn't run at all. Because of these physical dangers, added to the psychological isolation they created for Indian Island residents, Florence worked to make sure a connecting bridge was built.

For decades, the sisters spoke before the Maine legislature, organized committees, wrote letters, and circulated petitions. It would take until November 29, 1950—when Maine's governor officially dedicated the new bridge—for this part of their dream to become a concrete and steel embodiment of opportunity, but they endured as a family alliance, undaunted by setbacks and naysayers.

In her fascinating chapter about Lucy Nicolar, published in the collection *Of Place & Gender: Women in Maine History*, anthropologist Bunny McBride contrasts the different strengths Lucy and Florence brought to their shared endeavors, seeing Lucy's extroverted style as a complement to Florence's more self-contained reserve. She notes that Florence "was a quiet but firm presence, a careful thinker more likely to voice her views with pen than tongue. Lucy referred to her as the 'tribal scholar.'" Another of Florence's granddaughters, Emma Nicolar, describes Florence, Lucy, and Emma as "all dynamic women, married to very active and dynamic men." Florence's husband, Leo Shay, nicknamed "the manager," served two terms as the Penobscots' representative to the Maine legislature.

When the United States entered World War II, Florence and Leo joined the war effort at Boston's Charlestown Naval Shipyard. She worked in the office and he built boats. Their four sons were drafted—although they still did not have the right to vote. Charles, the second to the youngest, served as a combat medic. He landed on Omaha Beach and crossed the Rhine into Germany, where he was taken prisoner of war. While Florence was very patriotic and felt proud of her family's sacrifices, the political irony was not lost on her.

In the fall of 1945, when Charles came home on furlough, the family took the ferry to Old Town and again tried to vote in a small local election. It must have been an impressive sight: Florence and Leo, Pauline, Lucy and Bruce, joined by other family members. At the head of the line stood Charles Norman Shay: highly decorated combat veteran and former POW, in his dress uniform, studded with medals. Yet they were turned away. "Idiots don't have any right to vote in this state," election workers told them. Eight years later, however, in 1953, they finally won: Maine's Indians gained the right to vote without changing their tax status. "They were so happy and proud of themselves the day they voted in Old Town," recalls Florence's granddaughter Emma Nicolar.

Emma fondly remembers her grandmother for more than her political activism. Food was scarce, but Florence cooked huge dinners for her extended family. Everyone was welcome, including Emma, who often showed up at mealtime. Florence loved good china and set the table with nice cloths and glassware. She modeled gracious living for her granddaughter, as well as the hard work and motivation to earn everything she had. Well into her seventies, Florence was healthy and vigorous; she made baskets, played the piano, helped her family, and remained active on behalf of her Penobscot community. On May 24, 1960, she and Leo were setting up for the summer season at their basket shop in Lincolnville Beach when she suddenly suffered a lung embolism and died. She was seventy-six.

Born into a dynamic family, Florence Nicolar Shay adapted the lessons of her parents, creating a life rich in personal artistic expression as well as practical and hard-won educational, social, and political advancements for her people. Her son Charles, who married an Austrian woman and lived and worked in Europe for forty years, returned each summer to Indian Island. He now lives in the house his Aunt Lucy built, and he opens her teepee shop in the summer. In the teepee, which he renovated extensively, are heirloom baskets his mother made. In his house are fine objects she collected, music she listened to and taught him to love. "She was revered by her children, grandchildren, and great-grandchildren," he says.

Granddaughter Emma shakes her head in admiration when she thinks about her grandmother and her Aunt Lucy. Knowing what few resources the women had on Indian Island, she marvels at how they found the time and the nerve to accomplish all that they did. "They were radicals," she says, "smart enough and courageous enough to leave a history." Thoughtful by temperament, strong by nature, deeply principled, and proud of her heritage, Florence dared to demand rights for the Penobscot people. While she lived to see many improvements, she believed there remained much still to do. Quiet Florence was the driving force in her family, recalls Emma. "When she spoke, you listened because you knew whatever she said was very important."

MARGUERITE THOMPSON ZORACH
(1887–1968)

Avant-Garde Painter
of Robinhood Cove

*O*n her first day in Paris, twenty-one-year-old Marguerite Thompson attended an exhibition of paintings called the Salon d'Automne. It was a life-changing experience. Her very presence on the streets of Paris that fall of 1908 seemed unlikely, almost a miracle. Marguerite had grown up in Fresno, California, a dusty town in the San Joaquin Valley. A bright student as well as a talented artist, Marguerite had planned to study at Stanford University— her trunks had already been shipped—when her aunt, Harriet Adelaide Harris, sent her the money to come visit her in Paris. "Aunt Addie" was a retired teacher and a painter herself, who had lived in Paris since 1900. She not only looked forward to her niece's company but also hoped to expose her to European art and culture. Marguerite grabbed the chance.

It was a long, exhausting trip by train and steamship, but now, having just arrived in Paris and eager not to waste a moment, Marguerite entered the imposing Grand Palais on the Champs Elysées. Inside were over 2,000 pieces of art by some 640 artists. Marguerite

Marguerite Zorach in her studio, 1913

was awestruck. The Salon d'Automne, established in 1903 as an alternative to the official salon, exhibited works by artists dubbed "The Fauves." At the Salon d'Automne of 1905, a well-known art critic had, in disgust, called the artists "fauves"—wild beasts—and the name had stuck. These avant-garde artists—Henri Matisse, André Derain, and Maurice Vlaminck, among others—used dazzling colors, squeezed directly from the tube, and applied them with bold brush strokes. Colors clashed and canvases swirled with intense emotion. Instead of trying to capture the illusion of a three-dimensional world on a flat plane, the paintings highlighted their two-dimensional surface, as if calling out to the observer, "Look, I'm paint on canvas!"

Many visitors to the Salon d'Automne were shocked, even scandalized. But Marguerite gloried in what she saw. Something new was in the air—the thrill and the challenge of modernism. These paintings, particularly Matisse's, stirred her independent nature and questioning mind. In a career spanning sixty years, she would bring to life amazing artworks—from paintings to tapestries, from batiks to embroidered clothes and hand-hooked rugs—all of which evoked what Jessica Nicoll, former chief curator of the Portland Museum of Art, calls "her truly modern spirit."

Marguerite Thompson, the daughter of Winifred Harris and William Thompson, was born in Santa Rosa, California, on September 25, 1887. Her mother was descended from New England seafarers. Her father, raised a Quaker in Pennsylvania, became a well-known lawyer for the Napa vineyards near Fresno, still a pioneer town when the family moved there in the early 1890s. Marguerite's was a refined upbringing. In addition to attending public school, she and her younger sister Edith were tutored at home in French, German, and piano.

Life for Marguerite revolved around art. From an early age, drawing absorbed her time, and she filled many notebooks with her drawings and sketches. She also loved the natural world, especially camping with her family at Yosemite and in the Sierra Nevada Mountains. After graduating from Fresno High School, she took postgraduate classes for a year then taught at a rural schoolhouse near Fresno. She was enrolled at Stanford in the fall of 1908 when her aunt's telegram arrived, inviting her to Paris.

Aunt Addie had traditional art training in mind, no doubt, but Marguerite was drawn to more avant-garde work. After failing the entrance exams for the École des Beaux-Arts (she'd never sketched a nude from life), she took lessons at various places until she found the Académie de La Palette. Here she studied with a progressive Scottish artist, John Duncan Fergusson. Soon after her arrival in Paris, Marguerite visited the American writer Gertrude Stein, who'd gone to Christian Science Sunday school in San Francisco with her aunt. Although she didn't attend Gertrude's salon often, she did meet Pablo Picasso there, whose cubist work would influence her own.

During the next three years studying in Paris and traveling through Europe, Marguerite soaked up new ideas and experimented with color and shape as she explored what kind of artist she would become. She exhibited at the Salon d'Automne of 1911, where her paintings used the vivid colors and forceful outlines of fauvism. She befriended a young English woman artist, Jessica Dismorr, with whom she studied, shared a studio, and traveled.

In March of 1911, a fateful event took place at a morning painting class at La Palette—Marguerite met fellow student William Finkelstein, who would become her husband and life-long creative partner. William's family had emigrated from Lithuania when he was a boy and eventually settled in Cleveland, Ohio. He'd left school after eighth grade to apprentice with a lithographer and later attended night classes at the Cleveland

School of Art. After several years studying art in New York, he finally went to Paris in 1910.

William, two years Marguerite's junior and new to the Paris avant-garde, was impressed by her talent and bemused by her modernist thinking. In his autobiography, *Art Is My Life*, he described watching her paint "a pink and yellow nude with a bold blue outline." When he'd asked if she knew what she was doing, she made it clear "she knew—and that was the beginning. But," he added, "I just couldn't understand why such a nice girl would paint such wild pictures." Marguerite "didn't look just like everyone else or dress like everyone else," he noted. "Even then she made her own clothes. She wore a black silk turban on the back of her head with an enormous red rose in the center—a fascinating hat. . . . She was shy but sure of herself and gave the impression of character."

For her part, Marguerite considered William "quite tied down by things and ideas," someone who might become "a very good painter of the kind that just misses being an artist." Marguerite was William's guide to this new art revolution, free from the rules of the past. It was Marguerite who urged him to "be just as artistic as you have it in you to be." Over the next months the two friends fell in love.

On October 5, 1911, Marguerite left Paris with Aunt Addie for extended travels through Egypt, Palestine, India, Korea, China, and Japan, before arriving back in California in April of 1912. Struck by the natural beauty of the places she visited, she made sketches and painted landscapes. She also wrote frequent letters to William, detailing what she saw, as well as her thoughts about art and the life they wished to share. To make a little money, she published a series of travel articles in the *Fresno Morning Republican* and was known to write fine poetry as well as prose. Her seven months in Asia and the Middle East exposed her to new cultures, geographies, and styles of art, which affected her artwork profoundly.

Back in Fresno, Marguerite struggled with the constraints of middle-class family life. Her parents hated her modernist paintings and tried to lure her back into the conventional world of society parties and teas. But she longed for the creative freedom of Paris, and she missed William. In October and November of 1912, she held her first one-woman show in Los Angeles, followed by a December show in her hometown. But Fresno could not hold her.

On December 24, 1912, Marguerite arrived in New York. William met her train and they were married that same day. They decided to take a new last name together and chose "Zorach," William's original given name, changed to William by a teacher in Cleveland. Now, as Marguerite and William Zorach, they settled in Greenwich Village. In an artistic explosion, Marguerite painted colorful canvases as well as original designs on yards and yards of unbleached muslin to decorate their apartment.

Two months after their marriage, the Zorachs exhibited paintings in the Armory Show of 1913, which art historian Roberta Tarbell refers to as "a landmark in the history of the development of early modern art in the United States." William's work received no mention in the press, but Marguerite's use of color left one newspaper critic appalled:

> The pale yellow eyes and the purple lips of her subject indicate that the digestive organs are not functioning properly. I would advise salicylate of quinine in small doses.

Although some members of the public misunderstood and even ridiculed her work, Marguerite seemed unaffected. She was brave and clear about who she was and what she believed. She also had William's full support, and they continued to paint in the same studio, helping each other with canvases, with ideas, with promoting their paintings. Although they struggled financially, these were rich, exciting years, and their collaboration nurtured them both. They exhibited paintings in their studio as well as at galleries, and they were at the center of the avant-garde community of American artists in New York.

In 1913 the Zorachs moved to another apartment, on Washington Square, where they lived for almost twenty-five years. At Marguerite's insistence, however—regardless of how poor they were—they spent every summer "in nature," borrowing friends' homes in New York and New Hampshire. In March of 1915, Marguerite gave birth to their first child, a son named Tessim. In 1916, she was one of only seventeen artists selected to exhibit in "the Forum Show," another groundbreaking artistic event. Her work incorporated cubist fragmenting of objects as well as the bold colors of fauvism. The Zorachs spent that summer, and two others, in Provincetown, Massachusetts, where they designed and painted scenery for the Provincetown Players. In November of 1917, Dahlov, a daughter, was born in Windsor, Vermont.

After the birth of her children, Marguerite no longer had long stretches of uninterrupted time. While she never gave up painting, she did less of it than before. Instead, she turned her artistic energies to designing and making embroidered tapestries—she called them "tapestry paintings"—which engrossed her for the next twenty years. She delighted in the wonderful colors available in wool yarns, more intense and varied than those of oil paints. Using innovative modernist styles, she elevated traditional handicrafts to the level of fine arts. Of her tapestries she wrote:

They are like symphonies that move and develop and change and contain a lifetime of growth, of power, and tenderness; of sharp contrasts and delicate nuance. They are creations that satisfy the artistic desire. And there is physical work, that same fascination that keeps a sculptor chipping away stone until the form stands revealed.

In 1919, the Zorachs spent the summer in Stonington, Maine, where William helped Marguerite create an embroidered panel, "Maine Islands." Here began their lasting connection to Maine. The years 1919–1920 marked a difficult time for Marguerite, however. While visiting William's family in Cleveland that fall, she caught influenza and was hospitalized for two months. In April, the Zorachs arrived in California to visit Marguerite's family. They stayed almost a year. Much of that time Marguerite was convalescing and unable to work.

In 1923, the Zorachs bought a tumbled-down saltwater farm, built in 1820, on Robinhood Cove in Georgetown, Maine. It cost $2,000, which was given to them by family friends. Although winters were spent in Greenwich Village, this was Marguerite's true home. Often she would arrive in late April, before her husband finished teaching at the Art Students' League or her children's school year ended. She designed, planted, and tended beautiful flower and vegetable gardens. The Zorachs both taught at the Skowhegan School of Painting for a few weeks each summer. The family kept a cow and horses and hayed their own fields. They raised Dalmatians. Three or four art students, who studied with William, lived at Robinhood Cove. It was a full and busy life with many visitors and much outdoor work to do. Often in the fall, when William and the children returned to New York, Marguerite stayed behind until late October to paint and to put the house and gardens to bed.

Because the Zorachs believed that children were born with an innate desire to learn, which most education discouraged, they enrolled Tessim and Dahlov in New York's first progressive school, the City and Country School, which Marguerite described to her friend Jessica Dismorr as "more free and modern than any I know of."

In addition to her artistic gifts, Marguerite possessed great practicality. Whereas William was a dreamer, she was levelheaded and a skilled domestic manager. Family members say she could do anything she set her mind to—from haying fields and milking cows to fixing broken furniture and managing family finances. At times Marguerite seemed aloof, remote from even those closest to her, but, notes Tessim's widow, Peggy Zorach, it wasn't an aloofness born of disdain. She just seemed preoccupied with her own inner world. "Marguerite had a real twinkle," Peggy adds, "and a delightful sense of humor."

For Marguerite, daily life offered endless potential for creative expression, whether or not it took place at an easel. Her daughter Dahlov remembers a home more vibrant and interesting than any of her friends':

> Our walls were canary yellow; Adam and Eve were painted on one wall, with the snake winding down the tree. The floors were bright vermilion, and covered with rugs that my mother designed and hooked herself. She created large batik hangings and bedspreads, and every piece of furniture was decorated, each chair rung a different color.

Some critics have commented that Marguerite's art career, a flaming comet in the teens and twenties—parallel to or even surpassing her husband's—was somehow diminished by domestic obligations, children to care for, homes to run. It's true that after William turned to sculpture in the 1920s, his fame did over-shadow hers, but Dahlov insists that her mother never stopped painting or developing as an artist. No matter how shaky the family finances, they always seemed to have hired help, so that both Zorachs could work much of the day. "Whatever you put your hand to is a work of art," Marguerite believed. Her artistic energies were more diffusely directed than her husband's, and her work blurred the lines between fine arts and fine handicrafts. For many years the art world did not value her work as highly as it did William's.

There was also the question of temperament. More self-contained than her husband, Marguerite took what came her way; she didn't promote herself to the extent he did. "Father used to nag her to do more, to complete works," Tessim told interviewer Cynthia Bourgeault for a 1987 article in *Down East* magazine. "He always had faith that she was a gifted artist. But she couldn't be bothered with short deadlines and the politics of the art world."

In spite of her independent spirit, it must have been difficult at times for Marguerite to deal with the discrimination that women artists routinely faced. The Downtown Gallery in New York, which had exhibited the work of both Zorachs starting in 1927 or 1928, continued to show William until his death in 1966 but dropped Marguerite in 1934—a bitter blow. Marguerite was active in New York art circles, and, as president of the New York Society of Women Artists, advocated tirelessly for greater access to exhibitions.

During the 1930s and early 1940s, Marguerite did a num-ber of large tapestry commissions. Her work sold well and was in high demand. After finishing a 9-foot by 6-foot embroidered por-trait of the Rockefeller family, she moved away from handwork.

Her eyes may have started to bother her; also, she now had longer uninterrupted stretches of private time to devote to her work. In any case, during the last thirty years of her life, she returned to painting as her primary artistic pursuit. She often painted brightly colored landscapes from her travels, but most of them explored her adopted home, Maine. These were glory years as her own unique style flowered. Curator Jessica Nicoll puts it this way:

> With paintings like "Sunrise Robinhood Cove" (circa 1951), she seems to recapture the spiritual power and intuitive color sense of her canvases from 40 years before, but with the experience of having been a painter throughout those intervening years. We sense her thrill of the extraordinary beauty of reflections in the half-light of daybreak, especially the red-hot ball of sun as it ascends over the horizon to initiate a brilliantly-lit new day.

Although their artwork took them in different directions, Marguerite and William continued their creative collaboration until William's death of congestive heart failure in Bath, Maine, in November of 1966. In her seventies, Marguerite suffered a series of minor strokes, but she remained productive until the last year of her life. She died in New York on June 27, 1968, at the age of eighty-one.

Today, Marguerite is highly regarded not only for her modernist paintings but for her extraordinary textiles. In the last several decades, the art world has taken renewed interest in her work, thanks in great part to the dedication of the Zorach family—daughter Dahlov Ipcar (a Maine artist herself), son Tessim Zorach, and his wife Peggy. Though Tessim and Dahlov's husband, Adolph, have died in recent years, both Peggy and Dahlov still live on Robinhood Cove. They are neighbors, in adjacent old white farmhouses filled with vibrant paintings, rugs, and sculptures created over a lifetime. Marguerite and William's five grandsons have taken up the Zorach legacy as well.

For a young girl born to a proper nineteenth-century family, Marguerite's was a remarkable journey—from Fresno to Paris, from New York to Maine. Dahlov once described her as "independent and outspoken, a feminist ahead of her time. She was anti-establishment, anti-religious, pro-art, pro-creative." Her spirit was unique, her gifts truly modern. More than thirty years after her death, Marguerite remains an inspiration, full of creative fire, true to her own vision of what an artist's life well-lived might look like.

FLORENCE EASTMAN WILLIAMS
(1892–1984)

Working Woman, Clairvoyant, Beloved Matriarch

In 1943, in the middle of World War II, times were hard in Portland, Maine. But at night in the USO Club near the waterfront, Big Band dance music and the sound of laughter filled the air. The club was a bright light for young soldiers and sailors heading to Europe on transport ships anchored in Portland harbor. And one of the brightest lights there was Florence Williams.

Florence, nicknamed Flossie, was fifty-one, a hard-working woman with a family to support, ever since she and her husband had separated. But, looking at her, you'd never know she had a single care. She was a buoyant spirit, with beautiful dark eyes and long black hair. Only four feet ten inches with size 2½ shoes—always very high heels—she was a dynamo. As a hostess at the club, she greeted new arrivals, served refreshments, and danced with the servicemen, many barely out of their teens. They called her "Mom Williams." Those evenings, her most important task—and pleasure—was talking to these kids about home: their families, girlfriends, dreams. She joked and made them smile; she admired their photos and listened

Florence Eastman Williams (far right) with two of her sisters

to their worries as well as their hopes. Throughout the war, she invited one or two of them to Sunday dinner at her house on Anderson Street. Because food was rationed, it was a stretch to feed so many. But at her table, everyone was welcome, all backgrounds, all races.

"Thanks, Mom," they'd say when they left the Williams' house, hearts gladdened and bellies full of fried chicken.

But June, Flossie's fourteen-year-old, would feel hopping mad. "She's not your mom, she's *mine*," she would snap.

Now a woman in her seventies, June McKenzie just laughs and shakes her head at her teenage jealousy, the way her mother must have done more than sixty years ago. Long after World War II ended, the same young men who appreciated Mom Williams's hospitality continued to correspond with her, and if they happened to visit Portland again, they made sure to stop by Anderson Street. Flossie's love for people and her ability to empathize led to a lifelong penchant for inclusion, even when she herself might feel excluded.

Florence Eastman was born in Portland on September 15, 1892, one of Annie Barnett and George M. Eastman's five daughters. Longtime Portland residents, Annie's family was originally from Dutch Guyana (now Suriname), on the northern coast of South America, where family members owned a railroad and had other landholdings. Before moving to Portland, the Barnetts lived in Portsmouth, New Hampshire, for a few years. In the early decades of the 1800s, when they most likely arrived in Portland, its docks teemed with commercial fishing boats and clipper ships. Granite, lumber, and manufactured goods—all moved to and from the city's docks. A small but cosmopolitan African-American community, including many seamen who worked on sailing ships, grew up around India and Fore Streets, near the eastern end of the waterfront.

Flossie's family lived on Anderson Street at the base of Munjoy Hill, half a mile from the waterfront, in a house just "down the yard" from her paternal grandparents, Charles and Harriet Eastman. A short cement walkway, lined with forsythia, hollyhocks, and hydrangeas, led from one house to the other. From her grandparents Flossie learned family history, from the days when Charles Eastman was the clerk at the Abyssinian Church, built in 1828. Still standing today on Newbury Street, the Church is Maine's oldest—and the nation's third-oldest—African-American meetinghouse. In the decades before the Civil War, not only was it the only school for African-American children, it was also a "safe haven" on the Underground Railroad.

No doubt Flossie heard stories about the Railroad from her grandfather, such as the one involving a run-away slave whom he helped deliver to freedom. Charles drove a hack in Portland—a horse and buggy taxi. He also was a barber and a taxidermist. In addition, he sometimes worked at the Portland Club. The fleeing slave, pursued by his former owners and by the police, was smuggled out of the South on a ship bound for Portland. Although Maine (part of Massachusetts until 1820) had abolished slavery in 1783, the year the Revolutionary War ended, it was still against the law to harbor a fugitive slave from another state. In spite of this law—and the great danger associated with breaking it—Charles Eastman drove his hack late at night to the Portland Club, where abolitionists had hidden the man once he was sneaked off the ship. Charles helped the fugitive into his buggy's secret compartment, then traveled across town to the Abyssinian Church until arrangements could be made to spirit him across the Canadian border. This type of compassionate action influenced young Florence greatly.

Flossie grew up at the end of the nineteenth and the beginning of the twentieth centuries. Around 1900, Maine—"this whitest part of the country"—had a population of approximately 700,000, of whom only 1,300 were African-American. Her father, George Eastman, followed in his father Charles's footsteps. He drove a hack, did taxidermy, and owned a barbershop on India Street, serving members of the African-American community, unwelcome at white barbershops. Although racism was more subtle than in the South, rules of segregation were still clear and boundaries were carefully watched. At that time schools were open to all children, but there was prejudice in housing, employment, and social opportunities. The Eastmans owned their own homes, so Flossie grew up not knowing that kind of discrimination.

As a girl, Flossie was taught to sew, do fancy handwork, and cook. She was a diligent worker and talented with her hands. She went to North School on the top of Munjoy Hill, graduating from the eighth grade in 1905. That ended her formal schooling. During her childhood she attended both the Abyssinian Church, whose membership was dwindling, and the newer Mission, part of the African Methodist Episcopal Zion Church, founded in 1891. (The Abyssinian closed in 1917, when Flossie was twenty-five.)

Flossie was the middle of five sisters. Annie and Alice were older, Gertrude and Irene younger. Gertrude died of "quick consumption" during a flu epidemic when she was only eighteen. All of the girls except Flossie were very fair skinned, and she believed that her mother favored them because of this. In fact, Flossie felt that her mother didn't like her at all, but she adored—and was adored by—her father and her grandparents. In spite of her mother's harshness, Flossie was a happy child—bubbly, warm, and funny.

In 1912, Flossie fell in love with Mitchell Williams, also a Portland native. He'd attended Tuskegee Institute, an African-American university in Alabama, where he'd trained to be a mechanic. He owned his own garage, but Flossie's parents still disapproved of him. She believed this was because he was darker skinned than her own family. Nevertheless, the couple decided to marry in December of 1912. Flossie was twenty. Without her parents in attendance, the wedding took place at the AME Zion Church, now called Green Memorial. After the ceremony, Flossie went home to gather up her belongings; she found them on the front stoop, wrapped in newspaper.

At first the young couple lived on Portland's West End, but after Flossie's parents reconciled to her marriage, she and Mitchell moved to the family's Anderson Street house. Their first child, Dorothy (called Dot), was born in 1913, followed by four more girls: Edith in 1915, Eleanor about 1917, Helen in 1919, and Audrey about 1921. Next came Mitchell Jr., who died in infancy. George Eastman Williams, called Sonny, was born in 1925. During her next labor, a difficult one, hospital staff didn't treat Flossie in time and the baby died with the cord wrapped around his neck—the result of medical neglect perhaps caused by discriminatory attitudes. Flossie gave birth to a daughter, June, in October of 1929, followed by another son, also named Mitchell Jr., in 1933. The last children, a set of twins, Jean and Joan, came in 1935, when Flossie was forty-three. Both died during a flu epidemic, one at ten weeks, one at ten months. Less than two years later, her fifth daughter, Audrey, died at the age of sixteen. Of Flossie's twelve children, only seven lived into adulthood. Although her heart was broken repeatedly, she expressed no bitterness. She refused to dwell on what she'd lost; she simply carried on.

Flossie created happy childhoods for her kids. Her home was a center of activity, always full of children, her own as well as others. She was a great cook and sewed all the girls' clothes, making muffs and coats, doing fine embroidery. Her kids attended North School as she had done, and all of them graduated from Portland High School. When they were little, they walked home for lunch to find fresh biscuits baking. She would be outside, waiting, chatting with her neighbors over the back fence: Irish, Polish, and Italian immigrants. Hers was the only black family in a diverse neighborhood, but Florence was a friend to all. "She never said a bad word about anybody," June recalls. When the Karolewskis, Polish neighbors, went for their citizenship papers, Flossie stood up for them.

Flossie was a terrific domestic manager, creating a loving but strict household. She ruled with a natural, quiet authority, with love, laughter, and firm rules. You helped with chores, you learned to share. Dinner was always at 6:00 P.M. "Be there," and the children were. Flossie never hit any of them and her reprimands were slight when anybody acted up: "Behave" and "Be nice" were her favorites.

While Mitchell told the kids, "If anyone calls you anything but your name, smack him," their mother would disagree. "No," she'd say, "that's not right."

From childhood on, Flossie knew that she possessed an unusual gift: clairvoyance. Well known and well respected for her ability to predict the future, she refused to take money when friends and neighbors came to her kitchen asking her to read their tea leaves. Even strangers would knock on her door and beg for her guidance. Sometimes the gift must have felt like a burden. Her face would change. She'd see a bright light shining on the wall. "Something's going to happen," she'd say. Once, after Mitchell had taken up long-distance trucking, she ordered one of the kids to go to the garage and "tell your dad to look between the truck and the cab, something's not right with the coupling."

"You've got to hurry!" she once told June, sending her off running to the same garage. Flossie could see Mitchell, plain as day, climbing out of his truck after it burst into flames. But June arrived too late to stop him. The truck did catch fire. Luckily, Mitchell escaped through a cab window, just as Flossie had witnessed it in her mind's eye.

Growing up, her children sometimes found their mother's clairvoyance annoying, but they learned to trust her instincts.

"You don't want to do that," she'd tell one of them.

"Why?"

"Listen to me. You don't want to do that." And invariably she was right.

June remembers her mother saying, "Uh-oh," out of the blue. "Somebody's coming here and it's not good." Sometimes it might be the police, sometimes a friend was sick. Because they didn't always have a phone, most news—good or bad—came through the side door.

During the Depression, the Williamses struggled, as did almost every other family. In the summers, they'd move to Scarborough, then a rural area about 10 miles south of Portland, where they owned a few acres. They lived in a small trailer on a beautiful parcel of land and had a regular farm with a cow, pigs, and chickens. Flossie planted a huge vegetable garden, whose abundant harvest she canned and preserved. The kids helped to hoe and weed. Late in the summer, before school started, the pigs would be slaughtered so there'd be meat through the winter. Mitchell especially loved the farm, but it was hard for Flossie because she didn't drive and felt isolated, far from her Portland friends and church community. About 1940, when Flossie was forty-eight, Mitchell decided to stay in Scarborough year round, while she returned to Anderson Street. Although the couple separated, they never divorced.

Mitchell still visited the kids, but now Flossie needed to support the family largely on her own. These were tough, lean, lonely times, but she kept her spirits high for her children and for the young servicemen at the USO Club where she soon found a job. The older set of kids were now in their twenties—the youngest of that group, Sonny, was fifteen. June was only eleven and Mitchell Jr., called Skippy, was seven. To feed them, Flossie took all kinds of jobs, all physically grueling, some of the few available to African-American women. In addition to working at the USO in the evenings, rolling bandages and teaching dance routines to a girls' youth group there, she cleaned houses for wealthy people during the day, and late at night scrubbed floors and cleaned bathrooms at Scarborough Downs Racetrack.

Most of Flossie's children grew up and moved away, but June remained in Portland near her mother. While June was raising her own family, Flossie lived upstairs and helped take care of the kids so June could work. The grandchildren adored "Nanie." She was a powerful force, a grounding, a pole star. For a number of years, she shared a room with her granddaughter, Michele, who now observes that while most teenage girls might resent such an arrangement, she loved it because Nanie was such a supportive and positive woman. Another granddaughter, Merita, remembers the afternoon ritual of drinking tea with milk or cream in the kitchen with Nanie, who "could see pictures in the tea leaves left in the bottom of the cup." A second mother to June's children, Nanie also had a wonderful sense of fun. She liked to dance, recalls Merita. "She would call herself 'dancing-a-jig.' She was so cute to watch. Standing about four feet ten inches, she would grab the edge of her skirt and hold it up while she shuffled and kicked her high-heeled feet."

When Flossie had a spare minute, she liked to play the card game whist with her friends, and she was an avid member of an all-black women's group, The Misteray Club. She was also very involved with the Green Memorial Church. As a member of the Missionary Board, she collected food, visited the sick, and took care of the community's elderly. Not long after a 1965 fire at June's house, Flossie moved to Franklin Towers, a subsidized housing complex, to keep her sister Alice and niece Shirley company. By that time, in her seventies, Flossie had retired from the heavy domestic work she had always hated.

As the years passed, she remained youthful, the center of activity for her ever-expanding family. Well into her seventies, she took up ceramics and made lighted ceramic Christmas trees for all of her children and adult grandchildren. Her hair didn't turn gray until she was about eighty-seven. June, who worked at a bank, would walk home to see her mother every day. "If I was feeling down, she'd cheer me up."

"Nanie lived a long life well," her granddaughter Michele says. "She loved loving other people, and she loved being loved." Merita notes that her grandmother's gifts were enduring ones. "Nanie taught me that, no matter what, I was a child of God, and that He loved me and so did she. She taught me that I had worth, and that I should take pride in myself. She often told me that 'we came from royalty in Dutch Guyana.'"

On the morning of June 7, 1984, Florence Eastman Williams felt sick when she woke up. She died that same day, at the age of ninety-one. "Small in stature, big in heart" read one of her obituaries. Nicknamed "Mom Williams" by servicemen during World War II, she was truly everyone's mother. For her, race didn't matter, nor did ethnic background or social class. She was a strong, strong person who accepted that you alter your dreams as you go along. While her life wasn't easy, she refused to dwell on the negative. "How can we move forward?" was both her challenge and her legacy.

Sister R. Mildred Barker

(1897–1990)

"Hands to Work, Hearts to God"

*I*n 1903, when Mildred Barker was only six, her father died suddenly, shattering the family and dramatically changing the arc of her future. Mildred's mother, unable to care for her two children, sent her son off to a trade school and placed Mildred at Holy Land, a Shaker community in Alfred, Maine. In the early twentieth century, it was relatively common for the Shakers to take in orphans or, like Mildred, the children of destitute parents. At the time there was no Aid for Dependent Children, no federal, state, or local agency to help needy families.

Overnight then, the Shaker brothers and sisters became Mildred's new family. One of her favorites at Holy Land was an elderly sister named Paulina Springer, whom she loved dearly. Sister Paulina taught Shaker hymns and songs to Mildred. Even at a young age, Mildred had a natural aptitude for singing and a wonderful memory. She was quick, bright, and wiry, with big brown eyes that didn't miss a beat. And keen ears that didn't miss a beat, either. After listening once or twice to a song then singing along, she'd memorize both lyrics and melody. Mildred seemed to soak up songs at a gulp, the way thirsty soil soaks up rain. She also

Sister Mildred Barker

delighted in learning the pantomime gestures that often accompanied the older hymns.

As Sister Paulina's health deteriorated, Mildred was assigned to help tidy her room and wait on her. "It was my greatest delight to do it," Mildred said years later, "because I thought she was just an angel, nothing else." Soon, Sister Paulina was too weak to leave her bed, but her spirit remained loving and strong. At age ninety, she wasn't sick with any particular disease, she was just simply fading away. One September morning, close to the end, she asked to see the children, who visited her bedroom one by one. Mildred came last. Frail as she was, Sister Paulina smiled at Mildred and squeezed her hand. "Promise me you'll be a Shaker," she said.

Growing up Shaker didn't necessarily mean you would adopt the Shaker faith in adulthood. At twenty-one, you had a choice: You were free to leave the community or sign the Shaker Covenant and remain. Mildred was too young to grasp any of this, but she would have done anything Sister Paulina asked, and so, of course, she promised. After Mildred left the room, Paulina told one of her fellow sisters, "I'm not going to be here much longer. Two angels standing over by the cupboard door are waiting for me." She died a short time later.

It would take Mildred many years to truly understand what her promise meant and to fulfill it. Although she was only eight when Sister Paulina died, the elderly Shaker exerted a powerful influence lasting to the end of Sister Mildred's own long and remarkable life. Out of the thousands of Shaker songs Sister Mildred knew by heart, one with special significance, would always be "Mother has come with her beautiful song," which Sister Paulina had taught her so long ago. This was a "gift song," given to Sister Paulina by a tiny bird. The "mother" the song refers to is the founder of the Shakers, Mother Ann Lee, and it was her teachings that shaped Mildred Barker's life, giving it profound spiritual purpose and meaning.

Ann Lee, born in Manchester, England, in 1736, was the daughter of a blacksmith. During her marriage, she bore four children, all of whom died. From an early age, Ann was "endowed with uncommonly deep religious feelings," Sister Mildred would write many years later in her book, *The Sabbathday Shakers: An Introduction to the Shaker Heritage.* Ann Lee joined a small religious group in Manchester, led by James and Jane Wardley. This society was called, derisively, "Shaking Quakers" and then simply "Shakers" "because of their ecstatic and violent bodily agitation" during worship. Sister Mildred wrote that Ann Lee, while under the guidance of the Wardleys, "became more deeply inspired and was blessed with divine insight, revelations and prophecies." Soon the group naturally turned to her for leadership and advice.

But in England Ann Lee and her followers were bitterly persecuted for their beliefs. She herself was beaten, stoned, and often put in prison. In 1770 she received a revelation to go to America. Because they were so poor, it took four years before Mother Ann and eight followers could raise enough money to pay the ship's passage. They left Liverpool, England, on May 19, 1774, in a condemned vessel, the *Maria,* arriving in New York two-and-a-half months later, on August 6, 1774.

The United Society of Believers in Christ's Second Appearing wanted to return to the simplicity of the early Christian church, believing that Christ's second coming lived within each individual. To the Shakers, "God is the First Great Cause. God is all, including the source of the Christ life spirit." Theirs were radical beliefs. One-hundred-fifty years before American women gained the vote, seventy-five years before the Emancipation Proclamation, the Shakers practiced equality in every realm of life: social, racial, economic, and spiritual. They shared all property and lived celibate lives. They also were pacifists, to whom Abraham Lincoln gave conscientious objector status during the Civil War. Each Shaker community was governed by two women and two men, called Eldresses and Elders.

By the time Mildred's mother brought her to Holy Land, the number of Shakers in the society had been declining for more than fifty years. At its height in the 1840s, more than 6,000 members had lived in nineteen communal villages in New York, New England, and from Ohio and Indiana to Kentucky. The Shakers inspired many other utopian attempts—social experiments which tried to create ideal communities. They have endured the longest.

Ruth Jackson, Mildred's mother, had been raised a Catholic in Manchester, England, where Mother Ann Lee had lived before she came to America. It is not known exactly when Ruth herself came to the United States, but she married Mildred's father, James Powell Barker, an Episcopalian, whose own family had roots in Rhode Island. The couple settled in Providence. Here Ruth Mildred was born on February 3, 1897. She had an older brother, and there was also a younger sister, but she died in infancy. After James Barker's sudden death, grief swallowed Ruth, who had no means to support her young children.

Ruth had a cousin who had joined a Shaker community in southern Maine, and it was there, by prior arrangement, that she took Mildred by train on July 7, 1903. It was a blistering hot afternoon when the train stopped in the middle of a cow pasture, surrounded by hills. Driving a horse and wagon, Brother Stephen picked up the two and delivered them to a cluster of large houses across the field. In the office of Eldress Fannie Casey, Ruth Barker signed a paper called an indenture, meaning that the Shakers would now be Mildred's family. Ruth returned to Providence on the next train, leaving her daughter behind.

The sisters were kind and welcoming. They showed Mildred her new home and introduced her to the fourteen other girls with whom she would share a single bedroom in the Dwelling House. But she was terribly homesick. She just couldn't understand why her mother had abandoned her. For several days she'd walk out behind the Dwelling House alone to gaze out across the hills. Providence lay just over the hills, she thought, and she planned to run away, back to her mother, her brother, her home.

In spite of the first traumatic days, Mildred quickly adapted to her new life. Soon she felt both wanted and loved. Of Eldress Harriett Coolbroth, her caretaker, she later wrote, "She was the mother that I needed, and as a young child I thought there couldn't possibly be anyone any lovelier." Almost every night before bed, she would go to Eldress Harriett Coolbroth's room, where she learned Shaker songs. One of the first ones began with the words: "Come, little children, come to Zion. Come, little children, march along."

Often, as the months and years went by, Mildred would stop sisters while they worked—in the sewing rooms, in the laundry and kitchen—to ask them to teach her songs. Years later she said, "It was almost a passion with me to see how many I could learn." Mildred's was a happy childhood as she learned not only to read and write but to do all kinds of useful housekeeping and homemaking chores, including knitting, sewing, spinning, embroidering, and jelly-making. The Shaker motto was "Hands to work, hearts to God," and Holy Land was a bustling enterprise, as well as a peaceful place of worship and prayer. To supplement their farming income, the Shakers made "anything we could sell." In the summer, an elder would visit resort hotels at nearby beaches or in the White Mountains, where wealthy vacationers bought such "fancy-goods" as poplar boxes, long cloaks, and hand-knitted sweaters. No matter what the product—from chairs and tables to mail-order packaged seeds, dried herbs, and lady's sewing baskets—the Shaker name meant top-quality workmanship, since Believers strove for perfection in all they did. Shakers were also known for their creativity. Flat brooms, clothespins, metal-point pens, circular saws, washing machines, early wrinkle-resistant fabrics—all were invented by Shakers intent on finding more efficient, labor-saving ways to perform their daily tasks.

Although Mildred's formal education ended with the eighth grade, she was an avid member of the Beacon Light Club. At weekly meetings she continued to read literature, learn history, and write essays and poetry, which she loved. She also enjoyed cooking. In fact, while still only in her teens, she was a head cook at Holy Land.

For years, Mildred didn't hear a word from her mother. Then, in 1913, when Mildred was sixteen, Ruth reappeared. She'd been remarried and wanted her daughter to come home with her. But Mildred refused. The Shakers were her family and Holy Land her home. Surprisingly, perhaps, Ruth agreed to this, understanding how deeply her daughter loved the Shakers, so different from "the world's people," as they called non-Shakers. The two visited often and remained close until Ruth's death in 1951.

In 1918, when Mildred turned twenty-one, she signed the Church Covenant, the first step in fulfilling the promise she'd made to Sister Paulina Springer years before. Throughout these years, the Shakers' numbers continued to dwindle, as fewer and fewer of the "world's people" converted. In 1931, the Alfred community was forced to close. Thirty-four-year-old Sister Mildred and twenty other brothers and sisters moved to "Chosen Land," a Shaker community at Sabbathday Lake, Maine, founded in 1783. Mildred would live there for almost sixty years.

Although she hadn't quite recovered from a serious illness late in the 1930s, Sister Mildred embraced a new and sizeable challenge at Chosen Land: She took the community's teenage girls under her wing. Being in charge of ten girls' physical and spiritual well-being consumed her energies, but she thrived on the responsibility. Sister Frances Carr, in her wonderful memoir, *Growing Up Shaker*, credits Sister Mildred with creating a happy and productive entry into womanhood for herself and many other girls. "We never experienced anything except a great deal of patience, love and kindness from her," wrote Sister Frances. Whether the girls chose to remain Shakers as adults or not, many called Sister Mildred "mother" and visited her as often as they could in later life.

No doubt remembering her own teenage years, Sister Mildred loved the girls, made them laugh, helped them learn, and kept them busy. In her memoir, Sister Frances tells a story about testing Sister Mildred. On the first night at the Dwelling House, after moving up from the Children's House, Frances avoided answering Sister Mildred's question about whether or not she'd said her prayers. Sister Mildred expressed neither surprise nor anger; she simply asked, "Would you like to say them with me?" Thus began a tradition that would last for fifty years.

Sister Mildred had a gift for making work-time fun. Even during lean years, Sister Frances recalled, Sister Mildred would turn an evening's sewing tasks into a party—with Kool-Aid and sandwiches made of ground-up Spam, cut into festive shapes. On birthdays, she whipped up rich chocolate cakes. One Christmas, she sewed housecoats for her girls in their favorite colors. A talented seamstress, she made thousands of potholders and hundreds of aprons to sell at the Shaker store. Every Friday evening, she taught the girls Shaker songs, passing on the oral tradition she had lovingly cultivated, and on Saturday afternoons she enjoyed listening to opera on the radio while she sewed or knitted.

When the fancy-goods business fell off because of the Great Depression—which coincided with Sister Mildred's arrival at Chosen Land—she proposed that the Shakers start up another money-making industry: candy. She and Sister Jenny convinced the society to invest $1,000 on state-of-the-art equipment, and they studied the candy-making process in Portland. Soon, the Shakers were making and selling thirty-one different varieties—from taffy to filled chocolates, which Sister Mildred hand dipped herself. Candy production reached its height in 1941, but then fell off during World War II when sugar was strictly rationed. Sister Mildred's jellies and jams were always highly prized, and she was known to be fussy about ingredients. Right before picking time, she would stride through Chosen Land's bountiful orchards to select the apples she wanted for pectin.

In 1950, Sister Mildred, then fifty-three, was chosen to succeed Sister Prudence as a trustee of the Shaker community, a position she held until she died. As such, she was both a spiritual and a temporal leader. She also wrote three books and many articles about Shaker life. Soon she was traveling around the country, giving lectures and serving as a Shaker ambassador to the "world's people." As the Shakers' numbers decreased, she sometimes grew tired of questions about the future of the United Society of Believers, but she was always gracious. With wry humor she once said to a reporter, "When people tell me, 'Oh, you're a Shaker. You make all that lovely furniture,' I feel like a table or a chair." Shakerism, she made very clear, was more than a beautiful chair or a quaint white cap.

Humble and modest, Sister Mildred didn't boast about her accomplishments. In telling her life story to interviewer Ann Waldron, for example, she left out that she'd met composer Aaron Copland in Cleveland when he was celebrating his ninetieth birthday. "Appalachian Spring," Copland's famous ballet commissioned for Martha Graham, included several variations of the Shaker melody "Simple Gifts," and he had been eager to learn its history from Sister Mildred.

In June of 1983, the National Endowment for the Arts invited Sister Mildred to Washington, D.C. At a gala ceremony, she and fifteen other outstanding folk artists—among them blues singer and guitarist John Lee Hooker—received National Heritage Fellowship Awards. Hers, given for her mastery of Shaker music, was presented by renowned folk singer Pete Seeger. Sister Mildred was eighty-six years old. Inspired by the event, she surprised the audience with an unplanned rendition of Sister Paulina's "Mother has come with her beautiful song." While in Washington, she also sang at the Smithsonian. Many of these songs had never been written down or preserved on tape until she recorded them. Interviewed by the *Washington Post* for a story about the National Heritage award, Sister Mildred said:

> I'm just an ordinary singer. I never had a big training, mine is just the spirit, that's all. I didn't realize for a very long time how important it was, it was a feeling I got myself from the old songs, the music. It suddenly came upon me that I was keeping the tradition alive, which meant everything to me.

When Sister Frances Carr was asked to describe Sister Mildred for an article in *National Geographic* magazine, she said of her beloved mentor, caretaker, and friend, "She is the most perfect Shaker I have known. [She] epitomizes Shaker values: compassion, love, total dedication. No compromises here. She is rigorous, a drill sergeant of the soul."

Sister Mildred herself, quoted in the *Maine Sunday Telegram*, reflected on the discipline, strength, and spiritual devotion needed to "take up the Cross." Perhaps she was thinking of her long-ago promise to Sister Paulina Springer when she said, "We have to work for it. It takes years to do it . . . It means transforming your whole life."

Sister Mildred died on January 25, 1990, at the age of ninety-three. She is buried in the communal Shaker cemetery at Sabbathday Lake. Chosen Land, believed to be the oldest continuously operating religious community in the United States, is still an active Shaker village. Five sisters and brothers keep up Shaker traditions on their 1,800 acres of rolling hills, orchards, fields, and pasturelands. At their store, they sell books, CDs, herbs, and crafts, and guides give comprehensive tours of the historic meetinghouse and grounds. The Shaker library, formerly the schoolhouse, is open by appointment to scholars, researchers, and any others seeking to learn about the Shakers and their many gifts to the world.

And what of the future? "We're just a small group," Sister Mildred once said, "but it's something that the world needs and I'm sure it's going to pass right down through many centuries. I don't believe that it will be lost. We can use all the strength and all the faith that we have and keep it alive and pass it to those who come within our reach. It's God's work, and He will sustain it."

MARGARET CHASE SMITH

(1897–1995)

"A Ship's Figurehead in Proud Profile"

On June 1, 1950, the junior senator from Maine, Margaret Chase Smith, rose to address her colleagues. "I may not have the courage to do this," she'd told a trusted aide earlier that day, but there she was, the lone woman in the Senate, poised to speak her mind, and her conscience. At the time of her speech, the United States was consumed with anti-Communist crusading, whipped to excess by Wisconsin Senator Joseph R. McCarthy. At first, Smith had supported her fellow Republican's move to purge the government of Soviet spies and possible Communist party members, and she enjoyed the damage it did to President Harry Truman's Democratic administration. But over time, McCarthy's witch-hunting tactics and his lack of concrete evidence to support his increasingly wild assertions made Smith uncomfortable. Reputations were trampled; careers were ruined without recourse to court proceedings.

At a speech in February 1950, Joseph McCarthy had waved a piece of paper, claiming it contained the names of 205 State Department employees whom the secretary of state knew were

Margaret Chase Smith, 1964

Communist Party members, yet whom still held their security-sensitive jobs. When Margaret Chase Smith pressed McCarthy to divulge the list, however, he evaded her and did not produce any other solid proof of his claims. Although some senators, even those in his own party, privately questioned McCarthy's methods and his increasing power, they too were afraid of Soviet infiltration of the government—and they were afraid of Joe McCarthy's reprisals if they criticized him, so they remained silent. It was in this climate of fear, confused patriotism, and name-calling that Margaret Chase Smith stood up in the Senate chambers that June day in 1950.

> . . . Those of us who shout the loudest about Americanism in making character assassinations are all too frequently those who, by our own words and acts, ignore some of the basic principles of Americanism—
> The right to criticize;
> The right to hold unpopular beliefs;
> The right to protest;
> The right of independent thought;
> The exercise of these rights should not cost one single American citizen his reputation or his right to a livelihood nor should he be in danger of losing his reputation or livelihood merely because he happens to know someone who holds unpopular beliefs. Who of us doesn't? Otherwise none of us could call our souls our own. Otherwise thought control would have set in. . . .

It was only a fifteen-minute speech, delivered in such a soft voice that some senators, once they realized the subject, had to lean forward in their seats to hear it. Margaret never mentioned Joe McCarthy by name, but her intention was clear. At the conclusion of her remarks, her aide, Bill Lewis, handed out 200 mimeographed copies of her "Declaration of Conscience," which six other senators had secretly signed. Margaret's personal and political bravery that June day, her moral authority, independent nature, and refusal to be bullied into silence, catapulted her onto the national stage, where she would become one of the most influential women in American politics.

Margaret Chase was born on December 14, 1897, in the central Maine town of Skowhegan. Her parents, Carrie Murray and George Chase, christened her Marguerite Mandeline Chase at the local Notre Dame de Lourdes Catholic Church. Ancestors on her father's side were Puritan settlers of Massachusetts, who'd come to the frontier of Maine in the late 1700s to escape the political and religious control Boston exerted on its citizens. (Maine was part of Massachusetts until the 1820 Missouri Compromise.) On her mother's side, Margaret had Franco-American forebears, who had migrated south from Quebec, Canada. For a long time, such French-speaking ancestry was considered by some in Maine to be both a stigma and a political liability. Margaret was largely ignorant of that rich heritage until later in her life, when she embraced it.

During Margaret's childhood, Skowhegan was a small rural town of about 5,000, set on the banks of the Kennebec River, which powered shoe and wood-products factories. George Chase was one of the town's barbers. Until her marriage to George, Carrie Chase had worked at the shoe factory as a fancy stitcher, a highly skilled position. Because George suffered from terrible migraine headaches, he sometimes could not work, so to help the growing family survive, Carrie clerked part time at the local five-and-dime. Margaret, as the eldest of six children, was her mother's partner in caring for the house and her younger brothers and sisters: three boys and two girls, born over a fifteen-year span. Of her parents

Margaret later noted, "My father was a good father, but my mother was a wonderful mother."

School did not particularly interest Margaret, but the world of business did. While still very young, she asked for a job at the dime store where her mother sometimes worked. The owner jokingly told her she was too short and advised her to come back when she could reach the candy on the top shelf. Margaret took him seriously and when she could reach the shelf at age thirteen, he hired her to clerk there after school.

At Skowhegan High School, Margaret was so disgusted with studying Latin and history that in her junior year she chose to move from the academic track of courses, geared to students who planned to attend college, to the commercial track. She played on her school's girls' basketball team, which won the state championship in 1916. Nicknamed "Marcus" by her teammates, Margaret loved the game, the camaraderie, and the competition. At only five feet three inches, she appeared taller because of her erect posture. "She walks as if she were stirring lemonade within herself," a classmate commented in their high school yearbook.

In the business world, from early on, Margaret was tireless and ambitious, always looking for better pay and job advancement. This led her, at sixteen, to become a substitute night telephone operator, work she credited with improving her memory as well as keeping her up-to-date on town affairs. At the time, all calls traveled through a central switchboard. Someone would call the operator and ask to be connected to a particular person, using the name rather than a number. Margaret memorized the numbers and often listened in on conversations.

One of the people in town she came to know through her telephone company job was Clyde Smith, the First Selectman in Skowhegan, who, at age twenty-nine, had been elected its youngest sheriff. When Margaret sat on night switchboard duty, he'd call to ask her for the time and weather. When she was seventeen and still a high school student, Clyde offered her a better-paying job as his part-time assistant in recording tax information, and he arranged for her to take typing and shorthand classes at night. Clyde was handsome and divorced, a ladies' man, a seasoned politician, and twenty-one years older than Margaret. From the beginning, their relationship—whatever it may have been—caused Skowhegan to talk. In any case, they worked well together and enjoyed a mutual attraction.

After she graduated from high school, Margaret went right into full-time work. Her family didn't have the money to pay for college, and she was eager to make her own way. When the full-time telephone operator job she wanted didn't materialize, she spent half a year teaching at a rural school. During that time, she felt very lonely and isolated from family and friends. She also was not particularly fond of working with rowdy children. The moment the telephone company job opened up, she grabbed it and moved back to her family's house on North Street, where she lived for thirteen more years.

The 1920s were a lively time for young working women, and Margaret took full advantage. She continued to see Clyde Smith, which fueled perpetual gossip, but she also traveled with a wide circle of friends. She belonged to a number of women's clubs, which were popular at the time and founded for recreation, self-improvement, and solidarity. In 1922, when she was twenty-five, she helped organize a local branch of the Business and Professional Women's Club, for which she served as vice-president. She was elected its president in 1923. Public speaking—never something she did easily, nor did most other women, she felt—was one of the group's goals: "to get the girls to be able to stand up on their feet and say something," as she described it. In 1925, when Margaret was only twenty-seven, she became president of the club's state federation.

By this time, Margaret was in charge of circulation for Skowhegan's weekly *Independent-Reporter* newspaper, with a salary of $18 a week. During her years at the paper, the *Independent-Reporter* received an award for the largest circulation of any weekly in New England. Margaret was a go-getter, friendly, genial, patient, and very hard-working. While she considered herself "a girl about town" and a "semi-flapper" who cut her hair short and liked a good party, she never drank or smoked, and in fact, often preferred to work and advance herself rather than attend purely social events. In her fine biography entitled *Margaret Chase Smith: Beyond Convention*, Patricia L. Smith describes Margaret, with her high cheekbones and strong jaw, as resembling "a ship's figurehead in proud profile."

In 1928, Margaret changed jobs again, becoming the office manager at Willard Cummings' woolen mill in Skowhegan. She'd heard about the opening when Cummings himself came into the newspaper office to place an ad, and she'd boldly asked, "What about me?" Working for Cummings, she earned $50 a week, a fortune in Skowhegan's economy, especially for a woman. Although she felt overwhelmed by what was demanded of her and claimed she "went home and cried every night for six months," she was determined to master the job and did. One of Margaret's tasks was to do payroll and hand out checks to workers in the dye house and carbonizer room. Contrasting the pittance they received with Willard Cummings's vast wealth, she came to appreciate the plight of ordinary mill workers, who spent long hours in unhealthy surroundings, earning 26 to 28 cents an hour.

On May 14, 1930, at the beginning of the Great Depression, Margaret and Clyde Smith were married. She was thirty-two, he was fifty-three. In spite of Clyde's wish not to have two politicians in the family, Margaret ran for committeewoman from Skowhegan and won. In 1932, she gave up her job at the woolen mill and devoted the rest of her life to politics.

When Clyde was elected to the United States House of Representatives in 1936, the Smiths moved to Washington, where Margaret again asserted her independent nature. Instead of acting the part of decorative political wife, she insisted on managing Clyde's office and being paid for it. When he objected, she appealed to voters back in Maine, who signed a petition stating they'd as much voted for her as for him, and she carried the day. Because Clyde had already used up the allowance Congress gave him for paid staff, he paid Margaret $3,000 a year directly out of his own salary. In addition to being her husband's secretary, she also researched material for his proposals and speeches. Although married now, Clyde did not change his ways. Margaret apparently learned about his infidelities early in their marriage; she never spoke of them, however, and did not leave him. The two continued to be an inseparable political team.

Less than a year after his term in the House started, Clyde suffered a heart attack, but Margaret kept his office running smoothly while he recovered. In spite of concerns about his health, Clyde ran for and won a second term. In 1940, Clyde's health was so poor that Margaret ran in the primary in his place—expecting to withdraw when he regained his strength. But Clyde did not recover. After his death, Margaret found herself heir to the Republican nomination and won the election that November.

During the difficult and lonely months that followed, Margaret threw herself into the tasks of a new House member. She made herself known for her work ethic and perfect attendance at all committee meetings and House sessions—not just for her trademark white gloves and hat, which newspapers never failed to mention. But something else made Margaret stand out: her principled independence. Often, she opposed the positions of Republican Party leaders, which earned her strong criticism. Her loyalty, however, went unwaveringly to Maine people and their interests. While serving in the House, Margaret also became increasingly involved in military affairs, serving on what would become the Armed Services Committee. She visited soldiers and sailors stationed around the world and championed equal pay, equal rank, and equal retirement benefits for women in the military. She also helped found the WAVES (Women Accepted for Voluntary Emergency Service) and the Army-Navy Permanent Nurses Corp.

Back home, Margaret was a popular politician and vote-getter. In 1948 she entered the Republican primary for one of Maine's Senate seats, campaigning against Horace Hildreth, the incumbent governor, as well as two other powerful candidates. Against the odds, she won the nomination, though the Republican Party refused to back her in the general election. She didn't need the party's help, it turned out. Her low-budget, grassroots campaign was so successful that she earned 70 percent of the vote. She made history by becoming the first woman to serve in both houses of Congress and the first elected to the Senate in her own right.

At Margaret's side, in the roles of administrative assistant, campaigner, and life partner, was her aide, William E. Lewis Jr. Fifteen years younger than Margaret, Bill was a Navy man who devoted himself to her career, much as she had devoted herself to her husband Clyde's.

As a freshman senator, and the only woman among ninety-five men in the "most exclusive men's club in the world," Margaret did her homework and sought important committee appointments but generally kept her mouth shut until—in spite of political expediency—she decided that "something [had] to be done about that man," Joseph McCarthy. After her "Declaration of Conscience" speech, which she wrote with Bill Lewis, the entire country knew about Margaret Chase Smith. Controversy raged. Many applauded her courage and willingness to challenge McCarthy's reign of terror. Most analysts agreed that she was morally right but politically wrong. "I wouldn't want to say anything that bad about the Republican Party," wryly noted Democratic President Harry S. Truman the day Margaret delivered her speech. The next day, in a newspaper column, Bernard M. Baruch wrote, "If a man had made the Declaration of Conscience, he would be the next President of the United States."

Less than a month after Margaret's speech, however, on June 25, 1950, North Korea invaded South Korea, and the United States again went to war, further stirring anti-Communist sentiment around the country. It would be four more years before the Senate officially censured Joseph McCarthy, but Margaret's Declaration of Conscience speech marked the beginning of the end for McCarthyism. In the meantime, McCarthy himself set out to punish Margaret. First, he kicked her off the Investigations Subcommittee, an influential post, and saw to it that she was removed from the Republican Policy Committee. But she never backed down and never stopped speaking her mind. In spite of her clash with McCarthy, she managed to become a member of two important Senate committees: Appropriations and Armed Services.

Three more times she won re-election to the Senate—in 1954, 1960, and 1966—each time by a 70 percent plurality. If in Washington Margaret struggled with members of her own political party, her Maine constituents—Republican, Democrat, and Independent—loved her. Citizens in other parts of the country, too, it seemed, responded enthusiastically to her plainspoken, honest, sometimes hard-nosed, ethical stands. By this time, Margaret was used to breaking new political ground for her gender, but in January of 1964, she did something which would have been unthinkable even a few years before: She announced her candidacy for President of the United States. Six months later, at the Cow Palace in San Francisco, she became the first woman to have her name placed in nomination for U.S. President at a convention of a major political party. She didn't win the nomination—Barry Goldwater did—but she made a lasting impression on American politics.

After serving in the U.S. Senate for twenty-four years, Margaret finally lost a re-election bid in 1973. Although she retired from elected office at the age of seventy-six, she did not retire from public life. At her home overlooking the Kennebec River in Skowhegan, she began to plan for the Margaret Chase Smith Library, which opened in 1982. There she met with visitors, researchers, policymakers, and school children. She also lectured widely at colleges around the country, conducted public policy seminars, and wrote for newspapers and magazines. In addition she published two books: *Gallant Women,* a collection of biographies of American women, and *Declaration of Conscience,* which dealt with the workings of American government. During her lifetime she received ninety-five honorary degrees, and in 1973 she became one of the original inductees to the National Women's Hall of Fame. The Associated Press named her Woman of the Year in 1948, 1949, 1950, and 1957. Although she never called herself a feminist, her life exemplified equality and paved the way for countless women, not only from Maine but from around the world. Currently, both of Maine's senators are women, carrying on Margaret Chase Smith's legacy of public service.

In 1995, Margaret suffered a stroke, then caught pneumonia. She died at home on Memorial Day that year. She was ninety-seven years old. Her own words—unadorned and rich with Maine understatement—might serve as a fitting motto for her extraordinary life: "When people keep telling you that you can't do a thing, you kind of like to try it."

BIBLIOGRAPHY

MARGUERITE-BLANCHE THIBODEAU CYR

Acadian & French Canadian Ancestral Home. "Kamouraska History." www.acadian-home.org/kamouraskaenglish.html.

Acadian Genealogy Homepage. "'Tante Blanche' was heroine of Colonists' black famine." www.acadian.org/blanche.html.

Albert, Thomas. *The History of Madawaska.* Madawaska, Maine: Madawaska Historical Society, 1989.

Chassé, Geraldine. Interview by author. Madawaska, Maine, June 18, 2004.

Franco-American Women's Institute. "Tante Blanche Museum, Madawaska, Maine." www.fawi.net/tanteblanche.html.

KATE FURBISH

Agger, Lee. *Women of Maine.* Portland: Guy Gannett Publishing, 1982.

Bonta, Marcia Meyers. *Women in the Field: America's Pioneering Women Naturalists.* College Station, Texas: Texas A&M University Press, 1991.

Furbish, Kate. Kate Furbish Collection. Brunswick, Maine: George J. Mitchell Department of Special Collections & Archives, Bowdoin College Library.

Graham, Ada & Frank Graham Jr. *Kate Furbish and the Flora of Maine.* Gardiner, Maine: Tilbury House, 1995.

James, Edward T., ed. *Notable American Women 1607-1950: A Biographical Dictionary.* Vol. I, A-F. Cambridge, Mass.: The Belknap Press of Harvard University Press, 686–87.

Wiggins Brook Rare Plant Station. "Furbish's Lousewort (*Pedicularis furbishiae*)." www.ifdn.com/unique/wiggins/unique.htm.

ABBIE BURGESS GRANT

American Lighthouse Foundation. "Restoration of Burgess/Grant gravesites." www.lighthousefoundation.org/burgess.cfm.

BIBLIOGRAPHY

Clifford, Mary Louise and J. Candace. *Women Who Kept the Lights: An Illustrated History of Female Lighthouse Keepers.* Williamsburg, Va.: Cypress Communications, 1993.

De Wire, Elinor. "Abbie Burgess at Matinicus Rock's Twin Lights." www.sentinelpublications.com/abbie.htm.

Parker, Gail Underwood. *It Happened in Maine.* Guilford, Conn.: The Globe Pequot Press, 2004.

U.S. Coast Guard. Keeper Class Coastal Buoytender, Namesake Biography: "Abbie Burgess Grant." www.uscg.mil/hq/g-a/awl/bclass/wlm/ abbieburgessgrant.htm.

Women in History. "Abbie Burgess Grant." www.lkwdpl.org/wihohio/ gran-abb.htm.

LILLIAN M. N. STEVENS

Agger, Lee. *Women of Maine.* Portland: Guy Gannett Publishing, 1982.

Giele, Janet Zollinger. *Two Paths to Women's Equality: Temperance, Suffrage, and the Origins of Modern Feminism.* New York: Twayne Publishers, 1995.

Gordon, Anna A. *What Lillian M. N. Stevens Said.* Evanston, Ill.: National Woman's Christian Temperance Union, 1914.

Leavitt, Gertrude Stevens and Margaret L. Sargent. *Lillian M. N. Stevens: A Life Sketch.* 1921.

"Mrs. L. M. N. Stevens Passes Away at Her Home," *The Daily Eastern Argus,* (Portland) Tuesday, April 7, 1914, p. 1.

Portland Women's History Trail. "Our Lady of Victories Monument." www.usm.maine.edu/~history/newtrail.html.

Ward, Sarah F. *Lillian M. N. Stevens: Champion of Justice.* Evanston, Ill.: Signal Press, 2004.

SARAH ORNE JEWETT

Blanchard, Paula. *Sarah Orne Jewett: Her World and Her Work.* Reading, Mass.: Addison-Wesley Publishing Company, 1994.

Dupre, Jeff, prod. and dir. *Out of the Past.* Documentary Video. PBS.

BIBLIOGRAPHY

Jewett, Sarah Orne. *The Country of the Pointed Firs and Other Stories.* Garden City, N.Y.: Doubleday & Company, 1956.

Jewett, Sarah Orne. *The Youth's Companion.* Boston, January 7, 1892, vol. 65, no. I, 5–6.

Morrison, Jane. *Master Smart Woman.* Documentary Film. 1985.

Morrison, Jane, Peter Namuth, Cynthia Keyworth. *Master Smart Woman: A Portrait of Sarah Orne Jewett.* Unity, Maine: North Country Press, 1988.

Silverthorne, Elizabeth. *Sarah Orne Jewett: A Writer's Life.* Woodstock, N.Y.: The Overlook Press, 1993.

CORNELIA "FLY ROD" CROSBY

Elden, Alfred, "Fly Rod, Now 83, Famous Writer of Outdoor Stories, Was Maine's First Publicity Agent," *Portland Sunday Telegram*, December 19, 1937.

Hunter, Julia A. and Earle G. Shettleworth Jr. *Fly Rod Crosby: The Woman Who Marketed Maine.* Gardiner, Maine: Tilbury House Publishers, 2000.

Maine Public Broadcasting System. *HOME: The Story of Maine.* "Program 5: The Nation's Playground." www.mainepbs.org/hometsom/program5.html.

McCubrey, March O. "Diana of the Maine Woods: An Analysis of Cornelia 'Fly Rod' Crosby's Involvement in Women's Outdoor Sporting Culture." Master of Arts thesis, Bowling Green State University, 1995.

Verde, Thomas A. "First Lady of the Maine Woods." *Down East: The Magazine of Maine* (August 1998): 57–59.

Women's History Trail: Augusta, Maine. "Cornelia 'Fly Rod' Crosby." dll.umaine.edu/historytrail/site6.html.

LILLIAN "LA NORDICA" NORTON

Bangor Daily News. "Mainers witness to singer's return." www.bangor dailynews.com/news/templates/?a=10349.

Brockway, Wallace and Herbert Weinstock. *The World of Opera.* New York: Pantheon, 1962.

Glackens, Ira. *Yankee Diva: Lillian Nordica and the Golden Days of Opera.* New York: Coleridge Press, 1963.

Klein, Herman. *Great Women Singers of My Time.* London: G. Routledge & Co., 1931.

Marston Records. "Three American Sopranos: Lillian Nordica, Olive Fremstad and Ada Adini." www.marstonrecords.com/3_sopranos/3sopranos_ward.htm.

"Nordica Homestead Museum." *Maine Archives and Museums Newsletter* 3, no. 4 (November 2000): 7–8.

Suhm-Binder, Andrea. Andrea's cantabile-subito: A Site for Collectors of Great Singers of the Past. "Nordica, Lillian." www.cantabile-subito.de/Sopranos/Nordica_Lillian/nordica_lillian.htm.

JOSEPHINE DIEBITSCH PEARY

Friends of Peary's Eagle Island. "About Peary." www.pearyeagleisland.org.

Hobbs, William Herbert. *Peary.* New York: The Macmillan Company, 1936.

Letters: Josephine Diebitsch Peary to Robert F. Peary. March 1900 and April 3, 1900. Josephine Diebitsch Peary Papers. Portland: University of New England, Maine Women Writers Collection.

"Mrs. Peary Dead; Admiral's Widow," *New York Times,* Tuesday, December 20, 1955.

Peary, Josephine Diebitsch. *My Arctic Journal: A Year Among Ice-Fields and Eskimos.* New York: The Contemporary Publishing Co., 1893.

Peary, Josephine Diebitsch. *The Snow Baby: A True Story with True Pictures.* New York: Frederick A. Stokes, 1901.

The Peary-MacMillan Arctic Museum. "Josephine Diebitsch Peary." http://academic.bowdoin.edu/arcticmuseum/biographies/html/jpeary.shtml.

Stafford, Edward Peary. "Introduction to My Arctic Journal." www.pearyhenson.org/Myarcticjournal.

Tanguay, Corina. "Josephine Diebitsch Peary." Women and the American Experience. www.une.edu/mwwc/ams308/peary.htm.

BIBLIOGRAPHY

FLORENCE NICOLAR SHAY

Ghere, David L. "Assimilation, Termination, or Tribal Rejuvenation: Maine Indian Affairs in the 1950s," *Maine Historical Quarterly* 24 no. 2 (fall 1984), 239–64.

McBride, Bunny. "Princess Watahwaso: Bright Star of the Penobscot." Weiner, Marli F., *Of Place & Gender: Women in Maine History*. Orono, Maine: University of Maine Press, 2005.

"Mr. and Mrs. Leo Shay Observe Golden Wedding Anniversary," *Bangor Daily News*, January 27, 1958, p. 18.

Nicolar, Emma. Interview by author. Indian Island, Maine, December 3, 2004.

Nicolar, Joseph. *Life & Traditions of the Red Man*. Old Town, Maine: Penobscot Nation Museum, 2002 (Reprinted).

Penobscot Indian Nation. "Penobscot Basketry." www.penobscotnation.org/museum/benewabskiegbasketry.htm.

Rolde, Neil. *Unsettled Past, Unsettled Future: The Story of Maine Indians*. Gardiner, Maine: Tilbury House Publishers, 2004.

Shay, Caron. Interview by author. Indian Island, Maine, December 3, 2004.

Shay, Charles N. Interview by author. Indian Island, Maine, December 3, 2004.

Shay, Florence Nicolar. *History of the Penobscot Tribe of Indians*. Old Town, Maine: Florence Nicolar Shay, 1941.

MARGUERITE ZORACH

Bourgeault, Cynthia. "'Very Much Her Own Person.'" *Down East: The Magazine of Maine* (August 1987): 66–71, 102–3.

Ipcar, Dahlov. Interview by author. Georgetown, Maine, October 28, 2004.

Marguerite and William Zorach. The Cubist Years: 1915-1918. Hanover, N.H.: The University Press of New England, 1987.

Nicoll, Jessica, Former Chief Curator Portland Museum of Art. Interview by author. Portland, October 22, 2004.

Seligmann, Herbert J. "The Zorachs of Robinhood Cove." *Down East: The Magazine of Maine* (August 1958).

BIBLIOGRAPHY

Tarbell, Roberta. *Marguerite Zorach: The Early Years, 1908-1920.* Exhibition Catalogue. National Collection of Fine Arts, Smithsonian Institution, Washington, D.C. 1974.

Zorach Homepage. "Marguerite's Page." www.exitfive.com/zorach/marguerite/marguerite.html.

Zorach, Peggy. Interview by author. Georgetown, Maine, October 28, 2004.

FLORENCE EASTMAN WILLIAMS

Clough, Stan. *Zion Upon a Hill: Portland's AME Zion Church and Social Uplift in the Progressive Era.* M.A. thesis, University of Southern Maine, 1994.

Hoose, Shoshana & Karine Oldin, prod. *Anchor of the Soul: The History of an African-American Community in Portland, Maine.* Documentary Video. 1994.

McKenzie, June. Interviews by author. Portland, September 17, October 7, and November 9, 2004, and January 5, 2005.

McKenzie, Merita. "Unpublished reminiscence of her grandmother, Florence Eastman Williams." December 2004.

McKenzie, Michele. Telephone interview by author, November 14, 2004.

Price, H. H., "African American Settlements Crucial to Underground Railroad." *Maine Archives and Museums Newsletter,* February 1998, 3–4.

———. "Maine is on National Underground Railroad." *Maine Archives and Museums Newsletter,* November 1997, I, 16.

Rogers, Phyllis. Interview by author. Portland, October 18, 2004.

Visible Black History. "Blacks in 19th-Century Maine." www.visibleblackhistory.com/19th_century.htm.

SISTER R. MILDRED BARKER

Barker, Sister R. Mildred. *The Sabbathday Lake Shakers: An Introduction to the Shaker Heritage.* Sabbathday Lake, Maine: The Shaker Press, 1985.

Burns, Ken, dir. *The Shakers: Hands to Work, Hearts to God.* Florentine Films, 1984. PBS, 1985.

Carr, Sister Frances A. *Growing Up Shaker.* Sabbathday Lake, Maine: The United Society of Shakers, 1994.

BIBLIOGRAPHY

Davenport, Tom, dir. *The Shakers.* Davenport Films, 1974.

Newman, Cathy. "The Shakers' Brief Eternity." *National Geographic* magazine, September 1989, 176, no. 3.

Sabbathday Lake Shaker Village. "About the Community." www.shaker .lib.me.us/about.html.

Wertkin, Gerard C. *The Four Seasons of Shaker Life* (photographs). New York: Simon and Schuster, 1986.

MARGARET CHASE SMITH

Margaret Chase Smith Center for Public Policy. "Biography: Margaret Chase Smith." www.umaine.edu/mcsc/AboutUs/Bio.htm.

Margaret Chase Smith Library. "Expanded Biography." www.mcslibrary .org/bio/biolong.htm.

National Women's Hall of Fame. "Margaret Chase Smith." www.great women.org/women.php?action=viewone&id=146.

National Women's History Project. "Margaret Chase Smith: A Woman Pioneering the Future." www.nwhp.org/tlp/biographies/chase_smith/ chase_smith-bio.html.

Schmidt, Patricia L. *Margaret Chase Smith: Beyond Convention.* Orono, Maine: University of Maine Press, 1996.

Sherman, Janann. *No Place for a Woman: A Life of Senator Margaret Chase Smith.* New Brunswick, N.J.: Rutgers University Press, 2000.

Stockwell, Angela N., Herbert E. Paradis Jr., and Virginia Foster, compilers and editors. *What Can I Do for You: Margaret Chase Smith's Story.* Skowhegan, Maine: Central Maine Printing and Publishing, 1997.

Wallace, Patricia Ward. *Politics of Conscience: a Biography of Margaret Chase Smith.* Westport, Conn.: Praeger, 1995.

 INDEX

About the Author

Before her current freelance life, Kate Kennedy taught writing half-time at Portland High School for twenty years. She has also taught English as a Second Language (ESL) to adults, basic literacy, and Sudden Fiction. In 2001, her novel, *End Over End,* was published by Soho Press. Her short fiction has appeared in various small magazines, her nonfiction in *The Island Journal* and *Arts Everyday.* Other projects include writing a library discussion guide for WGBH-Masterpiece Theatre and editing the Maine Island Trail Association's annual guidebook. Currently, Kate is working on a novel set in the Southwest during the uranium days of the 1950s. She continues to present writing workshops around the state, as well as to lead book discussions for the Maine Humanities Council. Although she grew up in California and New Jersey, Maine has been Kate's home since 1977. She and her husband live in Cape Elizabeth, enjoying three (and sometimes four) generations of family within a 100-mile span.